INQUIRY INTO CRUCIAL AMERICAN PROBLEMS

Series Editor · JACK R. FRAENKEL

Country, Conscience, and Conscription:

Can They Be Reconciled?

MARION A. BRESSLER

Social Studies Department
Senior High School
State College, Pennsylvania

LEO A. BRESSLER

Associate Professor of English
The Pennsylvania State University

PRENTICE-HALL, INC.   ENGLEWOOD CLIFFS, N.J.

Titles in this series:

13-183806-7 paper
13-183814-8 cloth

2   3   4   5   6   7   8   9   10

Prentice-Hall International, Inc.,
London
Prentice-Hall of Australia, Pty. Ltd.,
Sydney
Prentice-Hall of Canada, Ltd.,
Toronto
Prentice-Hall of India Private Ltd.,
New Delhi
Prentice-Hall of Japan, Inc.,
Tokyo

109474

PREFACE

The series *INQUIRY INTO CRUCIAL AMERICAN PROB-LEMS* focuses upon a number of important contemporary social and political issues. Each book presents an in-depth study of a particular problem, selected because of its pressing intrusion into the minds and consciences of most Americans today. A major concern has been the desire to make the materials relevant to students. Every title in the series, therefore, has been selected because, in one way or another, it suggests a problem of concern to students today.

A number of divergent viewpoints, from a wide variety of different *kinds* of sources, encourage discussion and reflection and illustrate that the same problem may be viewed from many different vantage points. Of concern throughout is a desire to help students realize that honest men may legitimately differ in their views.

After a short chapter introducing the questions with which the book will deal, Chapter 2 presents a brief historical and contemporary background so that students will have more than just a superficial understanding of the problem under study. In the readings that follow, a conscientious effort has been made to avoid endorsing any one viewpoint as the "right" viewpoint, or to evaluate the arguments of particular individuals. No conclusions are drawn. Instead, a number of questions for discussion and reflection are posed at the end of each reading so that students can come to their own conclusions.

Great care has been taken to insure that the readings included in each book are just that—readable! We have searched particularly for articles that are of high interest, yet from which differing viewpoints may be legitimately inferred. Whenever possible, dialogues involving or descriptions showing actual people responding and reacting to problematic situations are presented. In sum, each book

- presents divergent, conflicting views on the problem under consideration;

- gives as many perspectives and dimensions on the problem as space permits;

- presents articles on a variety of reading levels, in order to appeal to students of many different ability levels;

- presents analytical as well as descriptive statements;

- deals with real people involved in situations of concern to them;

- includes questions which encourage discussion and thought of the various viewpoints expressed;

- includes activities to involve students to consider further the issues embedded in the problem.

CONTENTS

5 Is the Draft Fair and Efficient? 65

6 What Alternatives Exist? 87

Introduction

> "It should be the aim of a wise man neither to mock, nor to bewail, nor to denounce men's actions but to understand them."
>
> *Spinoza*

If you have watched news reports on television, you will no doubt recall such scenes as the following:

Scene I: The place is a cemetery. On one side of a flag-draped coffin stand the mourners; on the other side a squad of Marines in full-dress uniforms are fixed stiffly at attention. A clergyman speaks in somber tones of "heroism," of "sacrifice," of "service beyond the call of duty." There is the sharp metallic sound of rifle bolts being driven home; three successive volleys fired over the coffin shatter the stillness. The mournful notes of the bugler's taps drift across the cemetery. The flag is taken from the coffin, carefully folded, and presented to one of the mourners.

Scene II: The place is near the front in Vietnam. A group of soldiers stand at attention. A high-ranking officer walks in front of the group and delivers a short speech praising the heroic action of the men fighting for their country's cause. He then proceeds to pin a medal on each of the soldiers, shaking the hand of each man and commending him for his individual act of courage and distinguished service to his country.

Scene III: The place is a street in a large American city. A group of young men mill about a small fire. There is a confusion of sound and motion, a waving of placards bearing various slogans opposing war in general, the war in Vietnam, the draft, or the loss of individual freedom. Occasionally one of the young men walks to the little fire, takes a card from his wallet, and drops it into the fire. About the perimeter of the group, a small crowd has gathered, some to applaud the activities, others to jeer and to hurl insulting remarks.

Scene IV: The place is a foreign country. A small group of young American men are gathered in a scantily furnished room. They are being interviewed by a reporter. Each of the men tells his story: he has deserted his ship or his military unit to seek asylum in a foreign country. The reason he gives is that he is opposed to war, or that he is opposed to the current war, or that he is being deprived of his freedom by compulsory military service.

The thing that must be apparent to everyone as he contemplates these briefly described scenes is the startling contrast between the first two and the last two. It is hard to conceive of these events taking place at the same time and involving citizens of the same country. We have a view, first, of a funeral with full military honors, signifying that a man has made the supreme sacrifice for his country and that the country is grateful and regards him as a hero; second, of the decoration of fighting men for their devotion to duty and heroic action in behalf of their country. In contrast, we have, first, a picture of young men vehemently protesting the right and/or wisdom of the country's involvement in war in general, questioning the authority or justice of the government in demanding that they serve in the armed forces, or absolutely refusing to serve. Finally, we are shown a number of young men who have left the armed forces, seeking the protection of a foreign government. In doing so, they have put themselves into a most unenviable position: they may remain in the foreign country which has given them asylum and thus cut themselves off forever from their families, friends, and all that their country has meant to them, or they may return to the United States and face the severe penalties that an act of desertion brings.

A visitor to the United States from some other planet would no doubt be bewildered by these sharply contrasting, contradictory scenes. Such questions as the following would probably occur to him: What kind of people are these? Why do they do these things? Why is it that some men are honored for doing what other men resent doing or absolutely refuse to do? Can a people be so divided that they disagree violently on a matter which may involve the well-being of both individual citizens and the entire nation? Are there any clear principles, ideals, or standards to help these people determine what is right and proper? Isn't there something wrong when a country can, at the same time, have thousands upon thousands of men engaged in waging a war and other thousands openly and loudly expressing their opposition to military service?—or is there?

Although we may have opinions concerning some of these questions —and perhaps even some answers—the general problem of military service is so complex and so many-sided that it has become one of the most troublesome issues of our time. The prospect of having to serve in the armed forces has had a special impact upon the youth of the nation, since it is the young men who are most directly affected. There is an old joke about the only certain things in life being death and taxes. Now a third certainty has been added—for young men, at least—that of the legal obligation to serve in the armed forces.

For many, of course, there appears to be no problem—or at least they claim none. They simply answer the call when it comes. But for countless others the matter of military service presents doubts, questions, and problems that arouse intense emotional responses and put minds into turmoil. Youths are troubled by the necessity of having their education interrupted or of giving up employment and plans for the future direction of their lives. A young man may have religious beliefs that are opposed to military service; his conscience may rebel at the thought of killing. On the other hand, he may have certain convictions concerning patriotic duty, about the obligation of a citizen to serve his country. From one side his ears are filled with the loud cries of protest against military service; he hears such words as *immoral, unjust, inhumane, imperialistic,* and *criminal.* From the other side he is confronted with such phrases as "patriotic duty," "service to country," "resistance to aggression," and "maintaining the respect and power of the United States." On the placards of marching demonstrators he sees such slogans as "Burn Your Draft Cards," "The United States Is Committing Murder," and "Fight for Your Freedom Not to Fight." Counter-demonstrators remind him that he must "Resist the Communist Menace," that we must "Bomb Haiphong," and that we are fighting to "Free South Vietnam." In a strange reversal of attitude, the young man who resists military service is regarded as a hero in some quarters; in others he is called a coward or a draft-dodger.

It is no wonder, then, that youth should be confused, uncertain, and divided in its reaction to the prospect of military service. When the voices of the nay-sayers are as many and as loud as those of the yea-sayers, it is indeed difficult to be certain about the rightness of one's thinking and action. However, no one can or should try to avoid giving serious thought to certain questions and issues involved in the problem of military service. The problem is a grave one, for upon its solution may depend the future of countless individuals as well as that of the United States of America as a whole.

The problem has many facets and involves almost every department of our national life—social, political, cultural, and economic. Thus it might be broken down into an almost infinite list of questions. But for our purposes we shall confine ourselves to four rather broad areas: the arguments in favor of military service, the arguments against military service, the various attitudes toward the draft, and some proposed alternatives to the draft. Some overlapping and repetition seems unavoidable.

The problem is obviously one that cannot be reduced to a simple equation, and the various attitudes and questions and answers cannot be regarded as clearly right or wrong, as plainly black or white. There are many "grey" areas; something may probably be said in defense of or in objection to all the attitudes toward military service and the methods of selecting men to serve in the armed forces. Perhaps the problem will never be solved to everyone's satisfaction until there is no longer any need for a military establishment—in other words, until that time when we have reached a state of universal peace. But since such a prospect is a rather dim one, and since the United States at present finds it necessary to have many thousands of fighting men distributed over two hemispheres, the problem affects practically everyone, directly or indirectly. It therefore demands that we give it our most serious and intense study.

This book is intended as a guide to the discussion of the problem of military service and, hopefully, as an aid to coming to some conclusions. To achieve these purposes a chapter on the history of the problem is provided to enable you to understand more clearly the complexities of the issues presented. The main body of the book is a compilation of the views of various persons with respect to the problem of military service in general and the methods of recruitment in particular. These consist of expressions of opinion ranging from the sentiments of some of the Founding Fathers to statements by those most directly affected by military service—the youth of today. Finally, an appendix suggests additional sources which the reader may consult to inform himself about special issues or to study the problem in greater depth.

A History
of the Problem

2

"And you will hear of wars and rumors of wars . . ."
Matthew 24:6

Although TV, the radio, the newspapers, and public demonstrations have made us more acutely aware of the problem of military service and the draft, the problem is by no means a new one. War is as old as man. Prehistoric man used stones and a sling or a crude spear to do battle. As he advanced in intelligence and skill, man devised bows and arrows, the catapult, swords and sabers, and finally gunpowder to use against his enemy. In the last hundred years the arsenal of war has been greatly increased to include swift machines of destruction for use on land, on and under the sea, and in the air. Scientists have produced complicated mechanisms of combat ranging from rapid-firing automatic rifles to great missiles that travel thousands of miles and bombs that could conceivably destroy civilization.

Wars have been fought for many reasons. In ancient times men often fought simply for land to live on and to supply them with food. Many wars have been prosecuted in the hope of material gain; the kings of ancient empires frequently sent their armies out to conquer lands so that they might collect taxes from the people. The Crusades represented a kind of "holy war," waged to wrest ground held sacred by the Christians from the Moslems. Several European nations have carried on wars throughout the world to gain power and prestige. World War II, precipitated by Germany, was a war of conquest based on the idea of a super-race. Many nations have fought to spread what they considered to be a superior economic or political system. Most nations have maintained armed forces, and have sometimes gone to war, to preserve their security or to avert being attacked.

The importance which man has attached to war is evidenced in many ways. A large portion of our history books is devoted to the military, and many pages are filled with accounts of battle action and heroism. Throughout history we have paid tribute to the military hero; in fact, the word *hero* is probably more often associated with deeds on the battlefield than with any other human activity. The world's literature contains countless works dealing with war and the men who fought gallantly or turned craven cowards. Beginning with the sword-wielding warriors of Homer's epic poems and extending in uninterrupted progression through the knights in armor of the Middle Ages to the Twentieth Century G.I., the military hero has been immortalized in prose and poetry. The village greens of small New England villages as well as the great squares of large cities throughout the world boast countless memorials in stone and bronze to the heroes of battle. We honor the military man with medals and ribbons; we celebrate his return from battle with great parades and elaborate ceremonials; and we accord the veteran special benefits and privileges in recognition of his services. In some instances we have given the highest office of our country to men because of the stature they achieved as military leaders.

At the same time that men have resorted to war for various purposes and have glorified the military hero, there have always been those who have objected to war and to military service. As long ago as the Sixth Century B.C. the Chinese philosopher Lao-tzu wrote as follows:

1. He who with Reason assists the master of mankind will not with arms strengthen the empire. His methods invite requital.
2. Where armies are quartered briars and thorns grow. Great wars unfailingly are followed by famine. A good man acts resolutely and then stops. He ventures not to take by force.

Confucius preached a doctrine of sympathy based on a kind of Golden Rule principle: treat your inferiors as you would be treated by your superiors. Approximately a hundred years before Confucius, the Hebrew prophet Isaiah spoke eloquently of the reign of peace on earth and of the evil of war, which he saw as a punishment upon his people for their sins. With the coming of Christianity there appeared more definite and explicit injunctions against the use of force and making war: Christian scripture counseled peace, unselfish love, overcoming evil, and nonresistance. The earliest Christians, the first unequivocal pacifists, followed the example of Jesus and would rather let themselves be killed than resort to arms.

These Christian traditions and principles have been carried on by various pacifist groups who have opposed and resisted military service. The most important of these in modern times have been the Society of Friends, or Quakers, the Mennonites, the Amish, and Jehovah's Witnesses. Although the pacifism of all these groups has not been absolute, since some of their younger members have accepted military service rather than accept exemption as conscientious objectors, there continue to be in each of these faiths many who ardently advocate peace and refuse to serve in the armed forces. At the same time, especially recently, their pacifism and resistance to military service have been supported by other religious groups, as well as by some whose reasons for refusing to bear arms are nonreligious.

The United States came into being through war, and a considerable part of our rather brief life has been spent in warfare or in anticipation of war. In its efforts to secure men for military service, our government has resorted to a variety of measures, from complete reliance on volunteers to a universal military training law. And from its inception to the present, our country has had among its citizens some who resisted or refused military service, as well as some who questioned the justice or fairness of the various systems of recruitment that have been used. The following pages attempt to provide a brief history of the methods used by the United States to provide forces to fight in its most important wars, the degree of success or failure of these methods, and the resistance to military service and objections to the systems of recruitment. Since quotas for the Navy, the Marine Corps, and the Coast Guard have generally been filled by volunteers, this survey focuses almost exclusively upon the Army.

A Brief Survey of Recruitment in the United States

The first shots of the American Revolution were fired by the Minutemen of Massachusetts, a small group of rebels who organized themselves into a local militia. For a number of reasons, there was opposition to a regular standing army. On June 14, 1775, the Second Continental Congress sent out a call for volunteers to enlist for one year. These volunteers, along with the Minutemen, composed the first Continental Army.

Because of the commitment to short-term enlistments, General George Washington was constantly faced with the problem of maintaining an effective military force. The complexion of his army was constantly changing as men left, after a period of service scarcely long enough to season them properly, and were replaced by green troops. The Commander-in-Chief was also distressed by the fact that men did not find patriotism a sufficient reason for re-enlisting, and he therefore indicated in a letter to Congress on November 19, 1775, that some other means "besides love of country" would have to be found "to make men fond of the service" and to keep the army at a respectable strength.

The measure finally decided upon was a system of bounties. These ranged from as low as $4.00 to as high as $750.00, as the various states indulged in competitive bidding for volunteers. In time the states added the inducement of grants of land to volunteers. Congress also found it necessary to grant additional bounties. Despite these inducements, Washington was still unable to secure an adequate army. Men were reluctant to be separated from home and family by long distances or for extended periods of time. Desertions were so numerous that Washington offered a general pardon to all deserters if they would rejoin the army. These circumstances impelled Congress, in February 1777, to recommend that the states draft men for nine months of service. Some of the states used the draft as an excuse to enlist criminals, hoboes, and all sorts of nondescript persons. Maryland made "every idle person" eligible for service; Massachusetts even drafted deserters from General Burgoyne's army.

That these measures were insufficient to meet Washington's needs was dramatized by the agonizing winter of 1778, which Washington's army spent at Valley Forge. With the troops starving and freezing in their wretched quarters, and frequently deserting, the cause of the Americans looked dark indeed. Because securing recruits was impossible, Washington urged again and again that Congress lengthen the term of enlistment and initiate some form of militia draft. Such a draft was finally put into effect by Congress and by some of the states, but it was a most unpopular measure, and most states attempted to secure needed recruits through increased bounties. Although this device did procure some men for long-term enlistments, Washington was constantly obliged to exert effort to secure a stable standing army.

The history of the first effort of the United States to summon its manpower to fight a war is eloquently summed up by a modern historian:

The brutal truth is that only a select minority of American colonists attached themselves to the cause of independence with a spirit of selfless devotion. These were the dedicated souls who bore the burden of battle and the risks of defeat: these were the freedom-loving patriots who deserved the gratitude and approbation of generations yet unborn. Seldom have so few done so much for so many.[1]

In spite of much opposition, in 1812 the resolution for war passed in the House of Representatives by a vote of 79-49 and in the Senate by a vote of 19-13. Again the country faced the problem of recruiting an

---

[1] Thomas A. Bailey, *The American Pageant*. Boston, Mass.: D. C. Heath & Co., 1961.

army. The governors of Massachusetts, Rhode Island, and Connecticut refused to make their state forces available, since they felt that there had been no actual invasion of the United States. The Massachusetts legislature, through an organized "peace party," announced to the public that "If your sons must be torn from you by conscription, consign them to the care of God; but let there be no volunteers except for a defensive war." In Worcester County a convention of delegates from forty-one towns urged citizens not to grant loans to the government and contended that the governor, rather than the President, should be the one to determine whether the emergency was grave enough to justify a presidential call for the militia.

As in the Revolutionary War, a "volunteer army" was inadequate in spite of bounties offered to induce men to enlist. However, severe opposition was encountered in both Houses of Congress to a suggested draft of 80,000 men from the state militia. David Daggett of Connecticut argued that "This bill is not only unconstitutional, but it is unequal, unjust, and oppressive—utterly inconsistent with the principles of free institutions to compel any man to become a soldier for life, during war, or for a fixed term." [2] Christopher Gore of Massachusetts regarded the draft as "the first step in the odious ground of conscription . . . in a manner presumed to be the least disgusting. . . . The people readily discern that the next step will be for a conscription for any purpose and by any individual designated by the General Government." [3]

The Mexican War again proved the ineffectiveness of short-term enlistment, although the question of the need for conscription was not considered. On the way to Mexico City General Scott lost 40 per cent of his men because their enlistments had expired, and thus he had to wait for reinforcements while Santa Anna found some time to recover.

At the outset of the Civil War, President Lincoln issued a call for 75,000 militia to serve for ninety days and later a call for 42,034 volunteers to serve for three years, a proposal later ratified by the Congress. Men were offered all kinds of inducements to enlist: permission to remain with their original militia units, bounties by the local, state, and national government, state bounties to nonstate residents. "Brokers had their crimps in Canada, offering bounties that were never paid, kidnapping civilians, and tempting soldiers of the British garrison to desert—there were almost 50,000 Canadians enlisted in the Union Army. State agents scoured occupied portions of the South for Negroes, and obtained shiploads of

---

[2] Arthur A. Ekirch, Jr., *The Civilian and the Military*. New York, N. Y.: Oxford University Press, 1956.

[3] Arthur A. Ekirch, Jr., *The Civilian and the Military*. New York, N. Y.: Oxford University Press, 1956.

men from the poorhouses of Belgium and Germany, all of whom were credited to their state quotas. Federal officials were bribed to admit cripples, idiots, and criminals as recruits." [4] It is reported that one bounty-jumper repeated his operations thirty-two times, and it was calculated that in some instances men, by claiming local, state, and national bounties, could amass as much as $1000.

Finally, in March 1863, the North resorted to the first United States conscription law. Recruitment was under the jurisdiction of the federal government and administered by the military. All male citizens and de-clared aliens 20–45 years of age had to register. States could fill their quotas with volunteers, after which the federal government would draft from the lists of registrants. Since a man could avoid service either by securing a substitute or paying the government $300, the well-to-do could evade service while the poor were obliged to serve. No provision was made to exempt conscientious objectors, and even though they could claim exemption by a commutation fee, many Quakers were opposed to this idea. After many appeals, Congress made some provision by which conscientious objectors could engage in hospital work in lieu of military service.

As usual, there were those who favored and those who opposed the draft. Senator James Nesmith of Oregon, who believed that the draft should have been in use from the outset of hostilities, announced that conscription was necessary to impart the iron discipline needed to win the war. "Without that sort of discipline," he declared after criticizing the equality of officers and men in the militia, "no government in the whole world can succeed with its armies. Your armies controlled by Democratic [sic] sentiment are nothing but a mob, and never can be otherwise." [5]

The opposition in Congress to the draft bill was convinced that such a measure gave too much power to the national government. Anthony Trollope, the English novelist, who had visited the United States early in the Civil War, wrote as follows concerning the militia draft of 1862:

This conscription is very bad. Was it absolutely necessary? My feeling is that a man should die rather than be made a soldier against his will. One's country has no right to demand everything. There is much that is higher and better and greater than one's country. One is patriotic only because one is too small and too weak to be cosmo-politan. If a country cannot get along without a military conscription, it had better give up and let its children seek other ties.

---

[4] Samuel Eliot Morison and Henry S. Commager, *The Growth of the American Republic, Vol. I.* New York, N. Y.: Oxford University Press, 1937.
[5] Arthur A. Ekirch, Jr., *The Civilian and the Military.* New York, N. Y.: Oxford University Press, 1956.

Determined resistance to the draft continued as men were enrolled to fill various state quotas. Minor draft riots occurred in such cities as Boston, Massachusetts; Wooster, Ohio; and Rutland, Vermont. But New York City witnessed the greatest violence. A riot which erupted there lasted four days, causing $1,500,000 in property damage and 1000 casualties. A mob of foreign-born laborers rallied about the slogan "Down with the Draft" and laid siege to draft headquarters. Abolitionists and Negroes were attacked, Horace Greeley's *Tribune* office was stormed, and an asylum for colored children was burned.[6]

The history of Union recruitment, then, is one of varied and complex methods of conscripting men and soliciting volunteers, and of widespread opposition to the various drafts which were instituted. Only 46,000 men were conscripted and 118,000 substitutions procured—or six per cent of the Union forces. The volunteer system proved ineffective without the sharp spur provided by the threat of a draft. The problem was further complicated by the fact that there were over 200,000 deserters.

The South found a need to resort to a draft one year earlier than the North. As in the North, a substitution system was used, and slave owners with one or more slaves were excused from service. Confederate conscription agents were often careless in securing registrations, and they avoided areas that were known to harbor "Yankee-lovers."

In contrast to the practice in the North, the Southern draft law exempted ministers, conscientious objectors, teachers, railway employees, and others. As the Confederate position grew worse, substitutions were cancelled, and the law was extended to include men from 17–50. No draft riots such as those in New York broke out, but a kind of guerrilla warfare was carried on between draft dodgers and deserters and the Confederate troops who tried to apprehend these men.

Perhaps the most significant development with respect to recruitment during the Civil War was the passage by Congress of the Act of March 3, 1863. This act, which came after other measures such as the militia system and bounties had failed, for the first time put the control of manpower into the hands of the federal government without regard for States Rights.

After the Spanish-American War, the Army was reorganized. By an Act of Congress 1903, the militia was defined as comprising every able-bodied male citizen 18–45, and every declarant alien in that bracket. The Organized Militia consisted of the National Guard of the several states; all other members were considered part of the Reserve. When World War I broke out, President Wilson was convinced that in a national emergency, the United States must depend upon a trained citizenry

---

[6] For a detailed and vivid account of this riot see Lawrence Lader, "New York's Bloodiest Week," *American Heritage,* X, June, 1959.

and not upon a standing army. The National Defense Act of June 3, 1916, was passed before the actual declaration of war, to strengthen the regular army, the National Guard, and the Reserve Force. After the declaration of war, the Selective Service Act of 1917 was passed. In the beginning, all men 21–30 were to register. Later this was revised to include men 18–45. Exemptions were few. Aliens, the physically unfit, and conscientious objectors were permitted to serve in noncombatant capacities. The final choice of draftees was made by a lottery. There were 337,649 draft evaders, of whom 163,738 were apprehended.

Unlike the Civil War draft, the execution of the law was left up to the local communities through the creation of local draft boards. The President was authorized to establish such boards in each county of each state. Each board was made up of three or more members appointed by the President upon recommendation made by the state governor. A board member had to be a citizen of the United States, at least thirty years old, and a resident of the county he represented. He could not be a member of the Armed Services and received no compensation for his services. It was with these boards that each draftee had direct contact, a typically democratic procedure. Although these boards were responsible for recruitment of needed men, they were also made responsible for channeling through exemption the manpower of the United States into occupations that would serve the national interest. Thus, many registrants, such as students, teachers, and scientists, were deferred.

Since many Congressional leaders feared a repetition of the draft riots of the Civil War, every effort was made to convince the public of the necessity for the draft. No substitutions were permitted and the local draft boards were given full authority. The Creel Committee made an effort to convince the public of the urgency to free the German people from the tyranny of the Kaiser and "to save the world for democracy." The Espionage and Sedition Acts, in the name of patriotic loyalty, stifled all opposition to the war. Anyone who criticized the policy of the government was liable to be labeled as a "traitor" and many people were.

Thus, when the first registrants were enrolled, a national holiday was declared. Few voices of dissent were raised, although there were a number of parades in opposition to the draft in the larger cities before the actual day of registration. On May 31, 1917, two college students, Charles Phillips and Owen Cattle, were arrested for writing a pamphlet against the draft—a pamphlet that, incidentally, was never published—and for advising students to resist the draft by going to jail. Several minor riots occurred in Montana and Michigan, and a pacifist meeting was broken up in Madison Square Garden. In the summer of 1917 some fairly serious resistance was manifested in several counties in Oklahoma, allegedly fomented by socialist propaganda, but the police were prompt to quell the disorder and to arrest the leaders.

Men like Robert La Follette and George Norris spoke out against the draft law as a deprivation of individual liberty and freedom. On the other hand, Charles Eliot, former president of Harvard, maintained that "universal military service is a grave but necessary choice"; and R. Barton Perry, a Harvard Professor, wrote in the *New Republic* that "the terms were in no way contradictory and that conscription would not destroy the free individual."

The Supreme Court, in a series of Selective Draft Law cases, held that under the Constitution, Congress was given the power to raise armies and therefore it could legally construct and pass a draft law act. The Court further maintained that compulsory service was not "involuntary servitude" within the meaning of the Thirteenth Amendment.

It is clear that men *were* deprived of their civil liberties, and the courts unhesitatingly prosecuted violaters of the draft act. Socialists Victor Berger and Eugene Debs were arrested, and a Pennsylvania German by the name of Charles T. Schenck was arrested for mailing circulars urging draftees not to report for induction. Justice Oliver Wendell Holmes, Jr., laid down the precedent known as "a clear and present danger," which held that in time of peace such circulars were allowable, but not in time of war.

The attitude of those in authority toward conscientious objectors was seriously divided. Representative Carl Hayden, favoring temperate treatment of conscientious objectors, declared that his stand was

not so much for their sake as from a belief that, in order not to sin against principles of liberty those in authority should show a decent respect for an honest conviction, no matter how erroneous. It can be said with truth that it was only by firm and conscientious resistance to the will of the State that the political and religious freedom which we now enjoy was won. It is, therefore, the part of wisdom to recognize the larger expediency of tempering justice with mercy.[7]

President Wilson and his Administration, on the other hand, were not inclined to deal gently with conscientious objectors. Wilson reasoned that "it has seemed impossible to make exemptions apply to individuals because it would open the door to so much that was unconscientious on the part of persons who wished to escape service."

As had been true in previous wars, the Draft Act did not recognize objections to military service on grounds other than religious or pacifistic. Socialist Norman Thomas appealed to Congress to give consideration to those who opposed the war as unnecessary and unjust. In September of 1917 the Civil Liberties Bureau of the American Union against Militarism,

---

[7] *Congressional Record,* 65th Congress, 1st Session, 1898, 5901.

later known as the American Civil Liberties Union, took steps to help men evade the draft and the Espionage Acts. Conscientious objectors on religious grounds, who numbered more than 50,000, generally accepted noncombatant duties, but some 4,000 refused any kind of service. Eventually a special board was created to hear the cases of these men, and all but 450 were assigned to noncombatant service or released for industrial or agricultural work. The 450 were court-martialed and sentenced to prison terms, in some cases for as long as sixteen years. All in all, however, conscientious objectors were given sympathetic consideration during World War I.

After the alarming acts of aggression by Italy and Germany in the mid-thirties, President Franklin D. Roosevelt, beginning with a speech in January, 1938, tried to alert the American public to the need for increasing the military strength of the United States. But because of our policy of neutrality and an isolationist group in Congress, no action was taken, and Roosevelt was branded a "war-monger" in some quarters. However, with the ravishing of Poland in September, 1939, Congress declared a "limited" national emergency and provided for an increase of 17,000 men in the Regular Army. With the fall of France in June, 1940, Congress, for the first time in our history, enacted a draft act in the time of peace.

Known as the Burke-Wadsworth Bill or the Selective Training and Service Act, this law required that all men 21–35 register for the draft. The emphasis of the act was on training, the total number of men to be drafted not to exceed 900,000 to serve for a year or less with no service beyond the limits of the Western hemisphere except in United States possessions. In November, 1940, President Roosevelt appointed Dr. Clarence Dyskstra, the president of the University of Wisconsin, as the first Director of Selective Service. Upon his resignation, Lt. Colonel Lewis B. Hershey succeeded him in the post on March 15, 1941. After the attack on Pearl Harbor, all restrictions on where men could be stationed were removed, and the period of service was extended for the duration of the war plus six months thereafter.

In May, 1942, Congress set a precedent by establishing the Women's Auxiliary Army Corps to free men from noncombatant duty. Similar women's service units were set up for the Navy, the Marine Corps, and the Coast Guard, and some 216,000 women saw service in the various branches of the armed forces.

Unlike the Selective Service Act of 1918, the Burke-Wadsworth Bill provided for the exemption of men who objected to military service on religious grounds. Conscientious objectors could be assigned either to noncombatant service in the armed forces or to civilian jobs. However, Congress refused to pass any legislation giving consideration to those who objected to military service on other than religious grounds. As a result approximately 6,000 men were convicted of Draft Act violations and sentenced to prison terms. "Over 4,000 of these were Jehovah's Witnesses who were denied classification as ministers." [8]

Although there were a number of pacifist demonstrations, most people accepted the draft as a fair method of providing for the defense of the country. This fact can probably be attributed in part to the general consciousness of the immediate threat of the Axis powers and to the unprovoked attack on Pearl Harbor, which served to unite the country. Although many volunteered their services, the chief instrument of recruitment in World War II was the draft.

Immediately after World War II, as after former wars, the process of demobilization was begun. This was accomplished over a period of months, according to a point system which gave men credit for months of service and overseas duty. Those who had the longest period of service were discharged first.

Prompted by expressions of alarm at the rapid demobilization, President Truman requested Congress to extend the Selective Service Act for two years and then on March 3, 1947, recommended that the Selective Service Act of 1940 be discontinued provided there were sufficient voluntary enlistments to maintain adequate military strength. However, without Selective Service the armed forces fell from over 2,000,000 to below 1,400,000 by 1948.[9] Thus on March 17, 1948, the President requested Congress to re-enact the Selective Service Act which was passed on June 24, 1948.

An Advisory Committee had been appointed by President Truman in 1947 to devise a plan for Universal Military Training. However, the Congress rejected the proposal submitted by the committee on the grounds that a measure of this kind would inevitably lead to a violation of American rights and to what was described as "militarism." Other arguments against the plan were that it would not promote peace, that it would not prepare a man for military service, and that it was too costly.

The arguments of those favoring such a bill were that military training and discipline were good for all young men and that it would raise the level of effective citizenship. General George C. Marshall believed that a system of universal military training would maintain military strength without fear of a standing army, that its cost would be a minor consideration when compared to the current scale of expenditure of the United States, and that the existing situation demanded that the United States

---

[8] Arthur A. Ekirch, Jr., *The Civilian and the Military*. New York, N. Y.: Oxford University Press, 1956.
[9] Figures from *The Selective Service System, Its Concept, History and Operation*. National Headquarters, Selective Service System, Washington, D. C., September, 1967.

have at least some partially trained forces on hand that could be instantly mobilized.[10]

With the involvement of the United States in the Korean conflict, once again the draft was used to recruit men for service, although the President was given the right to call out the National Guard and the Reserve for twenty-one months. However, unlike World War II, this conflict required only partial mobilization and thus demanded greater selectivity on the part of the draft boards. Since an insufficient number of medical, dental, and allied specialists volunteered, on September 9, 1950, Congress passed a "Doctor Draft Law" to assure adequate medical and dental care.

The Selective Service Act of 1948 was extended by the Universal Military Training and Service Act of 1951. Once again Congress debated but never passed provisions for universal military training. The general sentiment in Congress seemed to be that such a proposal represented a subtle effort on the part of the Pentagon to move the United States away from its traditional policy of demobilization and disarmament and toward the creation of a permanent military establishment. In 1955 Congress did provide young men who had not reached draft age the opportunity of discharging their service requirement by serving three to six months of active duty and eight years in the Regular Reserves.[11]

On June 19, 1951, the Selective Service Act was extended to July 1, 1955, and later to 1963. The age limit was lowered to 18½, although every man was required to register at 18, and those 18½–26 were made liable for training and service for 24 months, except in cases of deferment or exemption. The President was empowered to induct as many men as he felt necessary to the maintenance of the strength of the armed forces. On March 28, 1963, the Selective Service Act was extended to July 1, 1967.

Prior to the build-up in Vietnam, there was considerable feeling that the draft was obsolete. Official studies indicated that the draft was wasteful and suggested that adequate manpower could be secured through a volunteer system if the inducements were sufficient. Thus, during the political campaign of 1964, President Johnson implied that the end of compulsory military service might be in sight. However with his election and the rising pressure for additional forces in Vietnam, this possibility was rejected in favor of a continued Selective Service. By June of 1966 the study undertaken by the Defense Department had completely reversed

---

[10] See William H. Young, *Introduction to American Government.* New York, N. Y.: Appleton-Century-Crofts, 1962.
[11] *How Can the United States Best Maintain Manpower For an Effective Defense System?* 90th Congress, 2nd Session, Senate, Document 75, Compiled by the Legislative Reference Service Library of Congress.

its 1965 position and argued that a voluntary army would involve pro-
hibitive costs—somewhere between four and seventeen billion dollars
annually.[12]

When the Military Service Act of June 30, 1967, expired, a new
law was put into effect on July 1, 1967, to extend until June 30, 1971. This
act empowers the President to draft 19-year-olds, and stipulates that all
conscientious objectors may be deferred on the basis of religion. Recently
the law was amended to eliminate deferment of graduate students, except
in the fields of medicine, veterinary medicine, and the ministry.

If there is one thing that this brief survey of military service in the
United States has shown, it is that the kinds of attitudes toward service
in the armed forces, problems of recruitment, and protests and demonstrations that occupy our attention today are really nothing new. The
problems which confronted Washington are essentially those facing the
President today. There have always been willing volunteers for military
service and dissenters of various kinds and degrees. The history of recruitment has been one of trial and error, of improvising, of devising,
modifying, and rejecting a large variety of systems. If the demonstrations
against military service and the draft make a greater impact upon the
public today than they did in 1865, it is mainly because television brings
them into our living rooms and the demonstrators have more efficient
methods of making their protests dramatic and forceful. However, although what we are experiencing is not new, it is more serious and complex. The United States is a great power in an unsettled, tension-filled
world in which military force is an accepted, or at least an effective,
method of settling international disputes. All the great powers of the
world have built up frightful arsenals, and there is a general consciousness
of the possibility of a holocaust. At the same time that there seems to be
great need for armed forces, there are intensified efforts to assure world
peace. The problem of providing for the military has become involved
with political, economic, and religious considerations, and the whole
matter of military service has been associated with the general question
of civil rights.

Out of these complicated and sometimes contradictory circumstances
have grown some extremely unrestrained and vitriolic protests against
the war in Vietnam, military service in general, and the draft. Public
demonstrations in the streets and on college campuses have involved
not only those eligible for the draft, but nationally known men and women
from all walks of life, ranging from figures in the entertainment world to
the clergy and members of the various professions. Young men have

---

12 Dorian J. Fliegel, "Forgotten History of the Draft," *The Nation,* April 10, 1967.

been publicly and privately urged to avoid the draft and counseled as to methods of doing so. Seemingly no person or institution has been immune to attack, from the military establishment to the President and the nation itself. Draft cards have been burned, the flag has been trampled in the streets, and the very foundations of our government have been challenged. At the same time, there have been counter-protests and marches in support of our military policy, we have continued to meet our draft quotas, and the strength of our military forces has not only been maintained but increased.

In view of these facts, it is important for you to attempt to approach the succeeding chapters with an open mind. The various opinions which are expressed should be viewed objectively and judged fairly. We must assume that these opinions are the result of honest conviction and that they therefore deserve our careful consideration. Above all, we are obligated to suspend judgment and avoid coming to conclusions until we have examined all the evidence.

What Do You Think?

1. From your reading of this survey of the history of military recruitment in the United States, what conclusions can you draw concerning the practicality of depending upon volunteers to fill the needs of the armed forces? What other attitudes seem to have existed all through our history?

2. How do you account for the problems that Washington faced in securing adequate forces to carry on the American Revolution?

3. In general, what seems to have been the attitude of many people toward the draft during the War of 1812?

4. In what ways did the system of recruitment used during World War I differ from that employed during the Civil War? Can you account for these differences?

5. Do you see any similarity between attitudes toward the draft during the Civil War and those often exhibited today?

6. What changes in attitude and position concerning the draft and the military establishment have occurred in the United States since 1940?

3

The Values of Service

"Dulce et decorum est pro patria mori."
(Sweet and becoming it is to die for one's country.)

Horace

Why should a man volunteer to serve in the armed forces or unquestioningly answer the call when he is drafted? Why should a man separate himself from home and family, disrupt his life and career, and risk grave injury or death on the battlefield? This chapter contains the most important and the most common answers that men have given to these questions. The opinions expressed range from those of seasoned veterans to those of 18-year-olds, from the highly patriotic to the purely practical. Perhaps you will be able to think of other reasons why a man should serve in the armed forces.

1. THE DRAFT IS GOOD FOR YOU *

How or why can the experience of serving in the armed forces "be the best thing that ever happened to a young man"? Here is what one man told his son in answer to this question, and what he would tell all young men of draft age.

Many a draftee looks forward to military service with about as much enthusiasm as he would to a jail term that could end in wounds or

---

* Excerpted from John Keats, "The Draft Is Good For You," *The Saturday Evening Post*, February 10, 1968. Copyright © 1968 by John Keats. Reprinted by permission of the Sterling Lord Agency.

death. Having spent four years in the Army myself, I must say that this is indeed what a military career in large part resembles. Therefore, whenever a young man tells me he was lucky to have escaped the draft, or that he hopes to escape it, or that he finds the Vietnam war to be immoral and says he does not want to go to it, I find his attitude entirely understandable—but absolutely wrong.

The whole truth of the matter must surely include these three facts:

First, we are moving, whether we like it or not, through the most murderous century in all recorded time, and we are at the center of world affairs.

Second, a tour of duty can be the best thing that ever happened to a young man. Granted, it can injure him, or at the very least waste years of his youth and delay his career—as it did for some 15 million men of my generation. Yet, in many ways that civilian life cannot, a military experience can also give a young man good reason to believe in himself and a realistic view of himself with respect to others around him.

Third, no one is lucky to escape the common experience of his time. Somewhere inside him, a man will always know that he has missed something important that everyone else has shared, and he will always wonder how he would have done, had he been there.

I think it necessary to keep these three facts in mind if we are to tell our sons anything sensible about the draft that awaits them.

*   *   *   *   *

I do not wish to sound like a recruiting sergeant, but the problem does exist, and our sons will be called upon to deal with it. If an 18-year-old boy thinks he can best defend the nation by being a conscientious objector, I have no quarrel with him as long as his objection is indeed conscientious and reasoned, and as long as he is willing to spend what would have been his draft term in alternate service that is in the public interest. But one way or another, I think the boy must realize that he has a civic obligation. (The boys for whom I have no use—and I have met several of them—are those who deny that they owe any sort of debt to their parents or to the nation that has so far provided them with a fairly fat life, and whose only objection to the draft is that they fear it would interrupt their pleasures.)

Now what happens to a boy when he is drafted? Today's Army, the one that my son entered, is basically no different from the one I entered at the time of Hitler's war, nor from the one my father entered during the Kaiser's war, and the first impressive thing about it is that it is a citizens' army, almost entirely composed of young men who almost certainly would rather be somewhere else. On his way to the induction center, the recruit is bound up in the kind of camaraderie that obtains in a pitching lifeboat, slowly pulling away from a steamer sinking in storm.

The mood of the incoming recruits abruptly changes to that of prisoners, however, beginning at the barbershop. The Army shears your scalp. You become part of a line of naked men to be examined, measured, fingerprinted, and inoculated against all manner of diseases. In the course of this shearing and stripping, the Army destroys all barriers between you and all the other men in the line; wipes away all your pasts and former conditions; does away with thoughts of college, jobs, aimless drifting, girls, worries, doubts, fears, ambitions. Then the Army thrusts you all beneath the level of manhood by dressing you in fatigue uniforms, and clad like jailbirds, you can only aspire to something better. A profound truth begins to emerge: It is the Army, and not whatever nation the Army happens to be fighting when you enter it, that is the first enemy of the soldier. You have entered an authoritarian society, insistent on its own peculiar needs, wherein all members of the society have only functional significance. Listening to the Uniform Code of Military Justice, you are struck by the repetition of the phrase, "shall be punished by death, or such other punishment as a court-martial may direct."

This is sobering. You, the recruit, are immediately confronted with the problem of personal survival—of survival as an individual. Civil life is too full of bypaths and hiding places, of protective families and friends, to provide the root-hog-or-die kind of confrontation that the Army presents. As nowhere else in our society, you are truly on your own. As a very wise drill sergeant put it to my group of infantry recruits, shivering in a Georgia sleet storm at four in the morning. "So far as I'm concerned, every one of you is equal until he proves himself different." This is not at all like school, where the teacher will try to find for every child some task at which the child can succeed. Instead, it is much more fair. You and all other recruits with hair as short, dressed alike, and equally ignorant of the new world you have entered, are given an equal opportunity to show what sort of men you are. You are set at common tasks. If you want to establish your difference from the men around you, it will be up to you, and you alone, to try it.

It is just here that you can, perhaps for the first time in your life, look around you to see how you measure up in honest competition with all other men. No parents are going to send you to a better school than other children attend; no one is going to give you a better job because of the influence of your father. You now have an opportunity to demonstrate your character, or lack of one. I will not say that you might not be given a chance to do so in civil life, but only that the Army gives you this chance in the bleakest possible way, and that you are extremely fortunate to be given this kind of opportunity on the very threshold of manhood.

Perhaps more fairly, and more desperately than in civil life, the Army searches for competence and rewards it by every means it can. After all, complex as the modern Army is, and comparatively few as its combat soldiers are, the Army is organized for the purposes of battle, and it is not anxious to trust incompetents with responsibility when failure to carry out that responsibility can cost not just money, but your life, or the life of the boy next door. The Army does not care about the security of the Army in which you are an anonymous cipher. I will not say the Army never makes mistakes about those whom it places in responsible positions, but I do say that if you prove yourself to be a better man than those around you, the Army will certainly promote you.

Promotion in the Army often gives you command of other men, and this can mean that you, only a year or two out of high school, can be given greater responsibilities and experience in handling other men than you could ever hope to be given in civil life at your very early age. Let us think about the 18-to-22-year-old age group for a moment. Labor unions do not want them in the job market, employers do not want them, and we do not want them hanging around the house. In fact, almost nobody wants them unless they are bright, and if they are, then we say that college is the only socially acceptable place for them. The other place, we say, is in the Army. We do not really reflect on whether college is necessarily the best place in the world, or whether the Army is some kind of junk heap, and few of us realize that the Army has lessons to teach that cannot be taught so well anywhere in civil life. I should say that one of the things the Army proves is that a 20-year-old-man, if he is a man, can handle a platoon, whereas civil life seldom gives anyone that young a comparable opportunity no matter how much of a man he may be.

The Army's standards are its own, of course, and therefore you will have to do what the Army wants you to do instead of what you might want to do. In a way this is limiting, and you may find it is oppressive, even stupid. But I am reminded that Robert Frost described writing free verse as being akin to playing tennis with the net down, which is to say that art implies performance within form. Military discipline and military rules comprise a very arbitrary form, and many a young man seems to be rather badly in need of some form within which to practice the art of growing into a mature person. I have seen too many confused college boys not to know how difficult they find the free-form civilian world to be, and I know too many parents who are thankful for what the Army has done for their sons not to know that discipline can be a kindness. Perhaps only after you have left the Army do you realize what it was all about. Perhaps some men never do understand this, but I should say that he who has undergone discipline will be better able to discipline himself.

But lest this sound too much like a recruiting poster, let us hear an enemy of armies speak. The voice is that of a Quaker, who, like all of his sect, believes that all wars are immoral and is opposed to all forms of coercion, including military life:

"I think we must all admit," the Quaker said, "that the Army is a creator of equality in our national life. It is, for example, one place where the Negro has a full, free and equal chance to move ahead, on the basis of his abilities, to middle-class status. It serves as a melting pot, bringing rural boys from the South together with boys from Wisconsin and Wyoming and the northern cities. It can be a kind of giant international-exchange program, in a sense, giving GI's and their wives and children a chance to live in another country in which they can learn to respect another people and culture.

"It is a place where lost kids can find themselves, and I will say I have seen young men, who were lost before they went in, come out of the service after a couple of years and go booming into civil life, full of drive and self-confidence they never had before."

Having served myself, I certainly do not believe that everything about the Army is good. For the most part I found my years in the Southwest Pacific boring, and I am sure that my son found his years in Oklahoma, Texas and Korea equally so. But I do know that it is a great source of satisfaction to learn that you can do what millions of men your age have done before you, and to have taken part in the events of your time. I also know that if you should be the one soldier in 10 who is told to fight, you will meet nothing on the battlefield that can be more hideous than anything other men have encountered before you. It is neither necessary nor possible for you to do better than the men who fought, say, at Gettysburg: You will merely be asked to do as well, and it is entirely likely that you will.

This is what I would tell a boy of draft age; this was what I told my son when it came his turn to decide just what his obligation to his country was. Much as I might agree with my Quaker friends as to the nature of wars and armies, I am more impressed by the fact that we are citizens of a great power living in a time of wars, and that maintenance of an Army is a sad necessity that has been thrust upon us. I am sorry about that, as an Army man would say. But that is the way it is. We need an Army, and someone must serve in it. Looking at any boy of draft age, I should ask him, "Why should it not be you?" I know what I am asking of him, but I also know that I am asking no more than has been asked of youth by any nation in time of war. And I know, too, that if he takes his turn in serving in the ranks, the Army, in its own relentless, uncaring and impersonal way, can be of service to him by giving him an opportunity to be himself, and that he will return to civil life more sure of himself, and feeling more certain of his right to citizenship, than anyone who has not served.

What Do You Think?

1. Do you believe, as the author says, that "the Army has lessons to teach that cannot be taught so well anywhere in civil life"? If you agree with the author, state what you believe these lessons to be.

2. Can you think of ways in which "discipline can be a kindness"?

2. WHAT IS A TRUE PATRIOT?

What, exactly, is patriotic duty? The following discussion of this question is based on the statements of prominent Americans, on some of the philosophical ideas in which the founders of this country believed, and on certain parts of our Constitution.

What is a true patriot? He is not simply a "solid citizen"—a man who pays his taxes, assumes a reasonable share of community responsibility, faithfully casts his ballot on election day, and takes off his hat when the flag goes by. He is not a man who does only what he must do for his country, who gives of himself only as much as he cannot avoid giving. The true patriot, recognizing the blessings and privileges his country offers him, is so completely devoted to his land that he will do and give his all to maintain and defend its glory. The true patriot realizes that no greater honor can come to him than that of fighting for—and, if necessary, dying for—his country on the field of battle. The true patriot also knows that in fighting and perhaps dying for his country he is only doing his duty as a citizen.

These are truths that have been recognized throughout the history of the United States. Some of our most eminent citizens have expressed them with fervor and eloquence:

Patriotism . . . this noble affection which impels us to sacrifice every thing dear, even life itself, to our country.
John Hancock (Oration, Boston, Mass., March 5, 1774.)

It may be laid down as a primary position, and the basis of our system, that every Citizen who enjoys the protection of a free Government, owes not only a portion of his property, but even of his personal services to the defense of it, and consequently that the Citizens of America (with a few legal and official exceptions) from 18 to 50 years of Age should be borne on the Militia Rolls, provided with uniform Arms, and [be] so far accustomed to the use of them, that the total strength of the Country might be called forth at a Short Notice on any very interesting Emergency.

>   *George Washington (From a letter to Alexander Hamilton.)*

I only regret that I have but one life to lose for my country.

>   *Nathan Hale (Spoken just prior to his being hanged by the British as an American spy.)*

Our country! In her intercourse with foreign nations may she always be right, but our country, right or wrong.

>   *Stephen Decatur, 1816*

. . . Loyalty means nothing unless it has at its heart the absolute principle of self-sacrifice. Loyalty means that you ought to be ready to sacrifice every interest that you have, and your life itself, if your country calls upon you to do so, and that is the sort of loyalty which ought to be inculcated into these newcomers, that they are not to be loyal only so long as they are pleased, but that, having once entered into this relationship, they are bound to be loyal whether they are pleased or not; and that loyalty which is merely self-pleasing is only self-indulgence and selfishness. No man has ever risen to the real stature of spiritual manhood until he has found that it is finer to serve somebody else than it is to serve himself.

>   *Woodrow Wilson (From a speech delivered before the Conference on Americanization, July 13, 1916.)*

Ask not what your country can do for you—ask what you can do for your country.

Let every nation know, whether it wishes us well or ill, that we shall pay any price, bear any burden, meet any hardship, support any friend, oppose any foe to assure the survival and the success of liberty.

>   *John F. Kennedy*

These are the words of true patriots, not of half-patriots. They are men who know that a nation can exist only when its citizens see and fulfill their obligations to the government. Their convictions are based on political thinking that goes back to John Locke, the seventeenth-century English philosopher whose writings on government furnished some of the most important guidelines for the framers of the Declaration of Independence and the Constitution. The most important idea of Locke's political philosophy is that of the social contract, or social compact. The laws of nature, Locke maintained, are good and designed for the happiness of man. However, because man has evil, predatory tendencies, he cannot live happily in the state of nature. Because man is what he is, he corrupts what might be an ideal society into one that is ruled by "jungle law"—by anarchy. To prevent this and to restrain his own contrary nature, man forms governments (a social contract). In doing this he voluntarily gives up his natural rights in return for the security which the government gives to his person and property.

What the half-patriots do not realize is that the government cannot give security to person and property unless citizens of the nation obey its laws and serve in its armed forces when the need arises. They do not understand, or they disregard, the fact that the government is an institution willingly created by the majority of the people, and that the citizen must abide by the will of the majority. Not to do so can only create anarchy—a condition in which there is no security and no freedom. Thus when our government, the creation of the majority of our citizens, passes a draft law, all able men are obligated to answer the call. No person can evade the draft, by whatever means, desert when he is drafted, or secretly or openly discourage others from serving in the armed forces and still claim to be a loyal citizen of the United States. As Captain Vere states in Melville's famous story *Billy Budd,* "We fight at command; if our judgment approve the war, that is but coincidence."

We might also refer those who would decide for themselves when or whether they will serve in the armed forces to the Constitution of the United States of America:

Article I. Section 8. The Congress shall have the power

11.   To declare war, grant letters of marque and reprisal, and make rules concerning captures on land and water;

12.   To raise and support armies, but no appropriation of money to that use shall be for a longer term than two years;

13.   To provide and maintain a navy;

14.   To make rules for the government and regulation of the land and naval forces;

15.   To provide for calling for the militia to execute the laws of the Union, suppress insurrections and repel invasions;

16.   To provide for organizing, arming, and disciplining the militia, and for governing such part of them as may be employed in the service of the United States, reserving to the States respectively, the appointment of the officers, and the authority of training the militia according to the discipline prescribed by Congress:

Article II. Section 2.

1.   The President shall be commander in chief of the army and navy of the United States, and of the militia of the several States, when called into the actual service of the United States;

. . .

Article VI.

2. This constitution, and the laws of the United States which shall be made in pursuance thereof; and all treaties made, or which shall be made, under the authority of the United States, shall be the supreme law of the land; and the Judges in every State shall be bound thereby, any thing in the Constitution or laws of any State to the contrary notwithstanding.

Here we have stated, in clear and unmistakable language, the powers of the government which the Founding Fathers thought necessary for maintaining the security of the nation. Few will deny that these provisions for national defense are not outdated. Only the half-patriots or the misguided will fail to recognize that these are necessary powers of government, that the will of the majority has granted these powers, and that they must be respected if we are to survive as a nation.

This does not mean that a citizen of the United States does not have the right to dissent, to criticize, to attempt to change a policy of the government with which he does not agree. It does not mean that a minority should be silent and passive. It *does* mean that the democratic process of majority rule must be maintained and that dissent must be kept within the limits of the law.

What Do You Think?

1. According to the quotations cited here, what seems to be the one indispensable characteristic of patriotism? Do you agree that it is indispensable? Explain.

2. Have you any answer to the argument that the Constitution is "the supreme law of the land" and must be respected and obeyed in order to maintain our security and freedom?

3. "DUTY, HONOR, COUNTRY" *

The following is part of a speech delivered by General Douglas MacArthur at West Point on May 12, 1962, upon the occasion of his receiving the Thayer Award for service to the nation. In this speech General MacArthur speaks of the importance and nobility marking the career of a soldier.

---

* Excerpted from General Douglas MacArthur, "Duty, Honor, Country," *Life,* April 1, 1964.

Duty—Honor—Country. These three hallowed words reverently dictate what you ought to be, what you can be, and what you will be. They are your rallying points: to build courage when courage seems to fail; to regain faith when there seems to be little cause for faith; to create hope when hope becomes forlorn. . . .

Every pedant, every demagogue, every cynic, every hypocrite, every trouble maker, and, I am sorry to say, some others of an entirely different character, will try to downgrade them even to the extent of mockery and ridicule.

But these are some of the things they do.

They build your basic character, they mold you for your future roles as the custodians of the nation's defense, they make you strong enough to know when you are weak, and brave enough to face yourself when you are afraid. They teach you to be proud and unbending in honest failure, but humble and gentle in success; not to substitute words for actions, nor to seek the path of comfort, but to face the stress and spur of difficulty and challenge; to learn to stand up in the storm but to have compassion on those who fall; to master yourself before you seek to master others; to have a heart that is clean, a goal that is high; to learn to laugh yet never forget how to weep; to reach into the future yet never neglect the past; to be serious yet never to take yourself too seriously; to be modest so that you will remember the simplicity of true greatness, the open mind of true wisdom, the meekness of true strength. They give you a temper of will, a quality of the imagination, a vigor of the emotions, a freshness of the deep springs of life, a temperamental predominance of courage over timidity, an appetite for adventure over love of ease. They create in your heart the sense of wonder, the unfailing hope of what next, and the joy and inspiration of life. They teach you in this way to be an officer and a gentleman. . . .

The soldier, above all other men, is required to practice the greatest act of religious training—sacrifice. In battle and in the face of danger and death, he discloses those Divine attributes which his Maker gave when He created man in His own image. . . . However horrible the incidents of war may be, the soldier who is called upon to offer and to give his life for his country is the noblest development of mankind. . . . Let civilian voices argue the merits or demerits of our processes of government; whether our strength is being sapped by deficit financing, indulged in too long, by federal paternalism grown too mighty, by power groups grown too arrogant, by politics grown too corrupt, by crime grown too rampant, by morals grown too low, by taxes grown too high, by extremists grown too violent; whether our personal liberties are as thorough and complete as they should be. These great national problems are not for your professional participation or military solution. Your guidepost stands out like a tenfold beacon in the night—Duty—Honor—Country.

You are the leaven which binds together the entire fabric of our national system of defense. From your ranks come the great captains who hold the nation's destiny in their hands the moment the war tocsin sounds. The Long Gray Line has never failed us. Were you to do so, a million ghosts in olive drab, in brown khaki, in blue and gray, would rise from their white crosses thundering those magic words—Duty—Honor—Country. This does not mean that you are war mongers.

On the contrary, the soldier, above all other people, prays for peace, for he must suffer and bear the deepest wounds and scars of war. But always in our ears ring the ominous words of Plato, that wisest of all philosophers, "Only the dead have seen the end of war."

What Do You Think?

1. Did you find this article effective? If so, was it the content or the style that affected you most? Explain.
2. This article sets the soldier apart from the civilian. Do you think this is a realistic distinction? Defend your answer.

4. THE CITIZEN AND MILITARY SERVICE *

One of the most vital questions with which we are concerned today is this: Does the world situation make it imperative that we provide for large armed forces to protect our security and freedom? A related, and equally important, question is, Just what part should the citizen-soldier play in national defense? A high-ranking Marine officer addresses himself to both questions in this article.

All debate, discussion, and theorizing with respect to military service is fruitless without an understanding of the requirements for an adequate military force in being.

No one, in his right mind, likes warfare. It is a brutal and expensive endeavor. It bleeds the nation of its life blood, and drains a nation's economic resources. Unquestionably, the nation's manpower and wealth, in the absence of war, could serve to achieve noble and constructive

---

* Excerpted from *The Forensic Quarterly*, 42, August, 1968, with the permission of the editors. Copyright 1968 by Charley Leistner. Written by Brig. Gen. Hittle.

Brig. Gen. Hittle, USMC (Ret.), is Director of the National Security and Foreign Affairs section of the Veterans of Foreign Wars of the United States.

gains. No one hates war more than the war veterans. No one under-
stands better its nature or, at times, its necessity.

But the hard, cold, and inescapable fact is that warfare has existed
almost continuously since the dawn of history. Just as there are things
in the street, there are international things who prey upon honest nations.

Just as laws do not dissuade the individual criminal, neither do
moral precepts, international law, nor appeals to reason, justice, and fair
play dissuade international aggressors.

Free men in free nations long ago came to the unpleasant and inescapable realization that to preserve freedom from those who would
destroy it requires military force. A nation must fight to preserve and
protect its independence from those who seek to destroy it.

Whatever section of the world one looks at today, there is ample
evidence that warfare in some form is a reality. Massive warfare remains a looming threat.

And let there be no mistake about it. The free world is under siege.
The power base of the free world is the United States. The United States
is the ultimate target of those forces which are today beating against the
ramparts of freedom.

An itemization of embattled or threatened areas of the free world
reads like a global geographic survey. In spite of all the talk about peaceful coexistence coming out of communist capitals, in spite of all the
happy theorizing and wishful thinking that communism has "mellowed"
and is really no longer a danger, the communist world and the free world
are still locked in a protracted struggle which communism has forced
upon us.

Anyone who doubts this is oblivious to facts, blind to what is going
on about him, and has departed from the world of reality.

For instance, Southeast Asia is torn by communist aggression. Hanoi
is waging the war of aggression against South Viet Nam, but it is the
heavy industry of the Soviet Union and the European satellites that are
providing the huge quantities of guns and ammunition that make the
massive aggression possible. It is added support from Red China that
gives even further backing to the cruel aggression.

In the Mid-East, the new Soviet Navy is the spearhead of Russian
expansion in the Mediterranean. Russian arms are flowing into the Mid-
East and North Africa. Russian missile-firing submarines are on regular
station in the Mediterranean, the sea flank of Western Europe. Also, the
Kremlin's missile-firing submarines are on regular station off the east and
west coasts of the United States.

Cuba still remains a communist base—supported and armed by the
Soviet Union—in the strategic heart of the Americas. Western Europe,
in spite of talk about Russian mellowing, is still a prime target of Soviet
expansion. Reductions in NATO military manpower have been matched

by increases in combat effectiveness of the Russian-commanded Warsaw Pact forces.

When in the summer of 1968, the United States began withdrawal of 35,000 United States troops from West Germany, there was hope expressed that the communists would follow our example and cut back their Warsaw Pact and Soviet forces arrayed along the Iron Curtain.

But such hopes were quickly turned to disappointment by the Russian response. Instead of matching our de-escalation, the communists took our reduction in force as a show of weakness and then took full advantage of it.

East Germany, on signal from Moscow, slapped travel restrictions and exorbitant freight rates on highway travel between East Germany and Free Berlin. This bold, but crude, act on the part of European communism, which in turn is the instrument of the Kremlin, was an inescapable reminder that the dangers to freedom are still threatening and that the communists are ready to pounce whenever they detect any weakening of our military strength.

So, history, as well as the reality of the present world situation, establishes the need for the United States, if it is to continue to live as an independent and free nation, to maintain the armed forces for defense of our nation. For the forseeable future these will have to be large forces. . . .

The term "citizen-soldier" should not be casually overlooked. It has tremendous meaning in the most practical sense. It can be said with accuracy that our nation could not have won its great wars in the past without the citizen-soldier. The same will remain true in the future.

The Veterans of Foreign Wars of the United States believes that the highest obligation of citizenship is the defense of our country. It cannot be relegated to only professional defenders.

The history of Rome provides persuasive evidence of the correctness of the VFW viewpoint concerning the citizen's obligation for national defense. As long as Roman citizens accepted and discharged their obligation to serve in the Roman army, Rome thrived and was secure. But as wealth and soft living eroded the Roman character, more and more citizens evaded military service. This trend continued until Rome was hiring mercenaries and placing the defense and the fate of the nation in their hands. The concept of the Roman citizen-soldier went out when dependence on the mercenaries came in. Thus, the decline of Rome became inevitable and its fall became a certainty. When Roman citizens no longer accepted the basic obligation and patriotic duty of taking, in their turn, military service in defense of their country, Rome was doomed.

In our time, a like danger exists. One of the most healthful contributions to our nation's continued existence, and the continuation of the American way of life, has been the large numbers of our nation's youth who have served in our armed forces and who have returned to civilian life. Because of their military service they have become mature, knowledgeable, and dedicated citizens. It can be said with good reason that service in defense of one's country is a proven school of good citizenship.

What Do You Think?

1. The writer contends that both history and the realities of the world situation today make it necessary for the United States to have large armed forces "for the forseeable future." Do you agree? Explain your answer.

2. Do you think that those who oppose military force are unaware of these realities or situations? If they are aware, what alternatives might they have in mind? How do *you* regard the world situation and how would you deal with it?

5.   WHAT SHOULD AN AMERICAN CITIZEN BE: RIGHTS AND RESPONSIBILITIES *

Can a man fully and properly discharge his duties as an American citizen if he is unwilling to serve in the armed forces? The holder of the highest office of one of our veterans' organizations answers with an unqualified no.

Having seen young Americans serving on both sides of the world, one cannot help but be impressed with the spirit, the capabilities, the know-how and the resourcefulness that American servicemen of today bring to the all-important job of defending freedom.

They are young Americans with a purpose and a sense of direction and, let's face it, while there are a lot of them who would rather be someplace else, they know why they are there, they recognize the need for being there, and you and I know they are fulfilling one of the most demanding responsibilities of American citizenship—that of bearing arms in the service of their country when such service is necessary.

If among them you should find an occasional bearded and unwashed individual it is because of circumstances, and not a matter of choice. When they get to hot water, soap and a razor, they remedy the situa-

---

* Excerpted from John E. Davis, National Commander, the American Legion, "What Should an American Be: Rights and Responsibilities," *Vital Speeches,* XXXIII, No. 8, February 1, 1967. (Speech delivered at the Los Angeles Bowl Luncheon, Los Angeles, California, January 3, 1967.)

tion—and I might suggest that all three of these necessities are readily available to most people here in this country.

Unfortunately, there are some among us whose need for cleansing goes beyond the physical. Their hearts, their minds and their moral persuasions need a bit of sprucing up, and they show it in their attitude toward their country and almost everything else that smacks of decency.

It was Alexander Hamilton who said: "Those who enjoy the fruits of democracy must be willing to bear arms in its defense," and, as I have mentioned I believe we are in agreement that this is the most demanding responsibility of citizenship.

Yet, it is a fact of life that there are those among us today who are all too willing to taste of the fruits of democracy and to enjoy the *rights* of citizenship, but who recoil in horror when it is suggested that they too must shoulder their share of citizenship *responsibility*. . . .

Citizenship is not a spectator sport. The strength of freedom and its very survival depends upon a thoughtful and active citizenry, and everyone who is concerned with his personal future, with that of his family and that of his country, had better get in the game.

We seem to be faced with a strange and unwholesome paradox today in that we are sending young Americans ten thousand miles from home to fight, and perhaps to die, in the cause of freedom, while here on the home front we are all too apathetic and lethargic about preserving the very virtues and principles for which we are asking these men to risk their lives. . . .

I suspect that one of the elements of that indoctrination that has escaped so many of our people is the American's Creed, written a half century ago by William Tyler Page, then Clerk of the United States House of Representatives. This is it:

I believe in the United States of America as a Government of the people, by the people, for the people, whose just powers are derived from the consent of the governed; a democracy in a republic; a sovereign nation of many sovereign states; a perfect union, one and inseparable, established upon those principles of freedom, equality, justice and humanity for which American patriots sacrificed their lives and fortunes. I therefore believe it my duty to my country to love it, to support its Constitution, to obey its laws, to respect its flag, and to defend it against all enemies.

*　　*　　*　　*　　*

Finally, we reach the ultimate demand of citizenship—to defend this country against all enemies. The American Legion believes it to be the responsibility of every able-bodied, mentally qualified, male citizen to bear arms in the defense of his country should the need arise. We do not believe that service in such areas as the Peace Corps or the Job Corps should be considered a substitute for military service.

An advertisement sponsored by Freedom House in the November issue of the New York Times lists a number of fantasies that should be renounced by the American people if we are interested in seeing the Viet Nam war concluded by a just peace.

Among them is this point: "That military service in this country's armed forces is an option exercisable solely at the discretion of the individual. No nation anywhere, now or in the past, has ever recognized that principle. Those who urge defiance on moral grounds merely betray the genuine tenets of conscientious objection which our people respect."

What Do You Think?

1.   In the third paragraph the writer suggests something more than he states directly. What does he suggest or imply? Do you think it is a fair suggestion?
2.   What does the writer mean by "a strange and unwholesome paradox"? Do you think it is unwholesome? Explain.

6.   THE POSITION OF THE VETERANS OF FOREIGN WARS OF THE UNITED STATES *

Is war still sometimes the only alternative for settling disputes between nations? The Adjutant General of the Veterans of Foreign Wars of the United States, while stating that war is a terrible and wasteful evidence of man's lack of social and moral progress, says that circumstances may still leave people who would be free no other choice but war. He argues that to refuse to serve is to shirk one's duty as a citizen and to defile the memory of those who have fought and died for their country, as well as the nobility, courage, and dignity of man. Would you agree?

Between his wars, man clamors incessantly of peace. Even famous generals profess to woo the "Dove," once their hands have grown too feeble to embrace the sword. Whether this be sheer hypocrisy, the dregs of personal remorse, or an honest attempt to curry favor with Divine Providence in their declining years, we cannot say. Yet for all of this, war appears on the records of human history to have been the most indispensable of man's group activities.

---

* Written especially for this book by Julian Dickensen, Adjutant General, Veterans of Foreign Wars of the United States.

It has been alleged by an army chaplain, who purported to quote from The Canadian Journal, that since 3600 B.C., the world we dominate as the most enlightened members of the Animal Kingdom has enjoyed just 294 years which were entirely free from the ravages of war.

It is estimated that man, in his evolution toward a civilized status, has disposed of approximately 3,560,000,000 fellow beings in the wars which he has waged. Further, that today, in a world in which innocent children are still starving as the direct result of abject poverty, it is possible to estimate man's total expenditures for war in terms of a solid gold band, one hundred feet in width and thirty-three feet in depth, which completely encircles the earth upon which he lives.

It would appear from these estimates that man's progress toward peaceful coexistence has been both troubled and slow; that his progress toward civilization has been costly indeed. When he can find nothing else to fight about, he goes to war over his differences of opinion concerning the most satisfactory technique for perpetuating peace.

Why, in the tragic and costly aftermath of war, does man repeatedly involve himself in others?

This is the question we must intelligently and realistically answer if we are to see the end of man's military history upon the earth. And only when we can be absolutely certain that we have seen the last of war can this nation or any nation lay down its arms and discard its military posture. . . .

It is not our purpose as an organization to decry peaceful attitudes or hopes, honestly and reasonably held. We do, however, condemn the self-destructive doctrine of peace at any price which beguiles the neurotic and completely selfish intellect of the frightened appeaser, or the designing reactionary.

It is these individuals, soliciting support from the craven and the weak, who insult the intelligence and kindle the resentment which grows and festers in the minds of normal men. . . .

Our members have fought to preserve this nation and the American way of life in six different wars. This was our personal and collective responsibility as American citizens. We view it as both a duty and a privilege.

We say this to all men: If indeed you feel the pangs of guilt and the need for self-degradation, wear your hair shirt in becoming silence. Repent your personal sins with some degree of human dignity. . . . Do not grovel at the feet of men. Do not shame or disgrace your country.

*   *   *   *   *

When peaceful efforts to resolve a continuing and aggressive threat to the rights of others have failed, war may indeed become the only honorable and acceptable alternative to slavery. In this event, it also becomes the only course consistent with man's self-respect.

Because of this unhappy tradition, together with the recurring mania of conquest, people who would remain free have no alternative but to maintain a military establishment adequate to the defense of their national sovereignty. It is for this reason, and no other, that we Americans establish and support professional military forces. Young men whose interests and ambitions so direct them, voluntarily elect to enter the "honorable profession of arms"—and thus commit themselves to fight our wars for us.

Since we deem their service essential to the nation as a whole, and because it leaves the vast majority of us free to pursue our own interests and ambitions, we routinely recognize their maintenance as a proper charge upon the public treasury. We educate and train them. We guarantee them job security and reasonable compensation. We provide them with numerous fringe benefits—medical and hospital services for themselves and their families, both during active duty and after retirement. We pay them substantial pensions, and authorize retirement at an early age. We then offer them civilian employment which enables them to capitalize upon their military skills, as well as their military service—without the loss of pension or of medical and hospital benefits.

This is as it should be. When the people of a nation, in order to pursue their own ambitions and to avoid the rigors and the dangers of war, prevail upon those who are willing to fight to go to war in their stead, they naturally expect to pay for their service. . . .

This nation's military history in time of war is not the history of professional soldiers. It is the history of civilians whose interests and ambitions were completely alien to the ways of war.

Civilian soldiers fired the "shot heard round the world" at Lexington and Concord. They wrested an infant nation from the British professionals at Philadelphia and Yorktown. Civilians manned the cotton bales at New Orleans in 1812. It was civilians who achieved immortality at the Alamo. Civilian soldiers, on both sides, wrote the bloody and heroic pages of the War Between the States. The Spanish War was fought and won by civilian volunteers. Both World Wars and the Korean Conflict added volumes to the colossal history of the heroism and effectiveness of civilians in the art of war. Civilian soldiers, marines, and sailors are again in combat in the jungles of Vietnam. . . .

The vast majority of our [the VFW] members were civilian soldiers. They are men who sought by choice to walk the roads of peace. They were content in youth, to leave the military role to others. But they were loyal, devoted, patriotic citizens. And having found it essential in six wars to take up the sword themselves to preserve freedom in the world, of which this nation is part, they have earned the right to be heard on matters pertaining to the welfare and security of this nation.

Be he pacifist or dreamer, religious zealot or reformer, crusader or disarmament addict; be his motives genuine or ulterior, he who would belittle the cause, the purpose, the faith, or defile the memory of the least of those who died, defiles also the nobility, the courage, and the dignity of unselfish man—and the cause of human justice.

This is the position of the Veterans of Foreign Wars of the United States on military service.

What Do You Think?

1. According to the author, what kind of people are those who support the doctrine of "Peace at any price"? Do you agree with his opinion? Explain your answer.
2. What point is the author trying to make by calling attention to the fact that our wars have been fought by civilian rather than professional soldiers?

7. REASONS FOR SERVING

You should find the following statements of reasons for serving in the armed forces especially interesting. The first was written by a teenager who was recently admitted to West Point, the second by a young man who has just reenlisted.

Why I Am in the Army*

Today's controversy over our presence in Vietnam is but one more episode in the age-old struggle between overt patriotism (or as its opponents retort—chauvinism) and civil disobedience. Should a young man consent to fight a war in which he does not believe, or is it his moral obligation to live by his conscience?

The transformation from anarchy to a governed society, whether democratic, socialistic or communistic, involves not only the attainment of certain rights and privileges, but also adherence to laws made by the elected representatives of the society. Although the individual may lose a portion of his freedom in this process, the benefits derived will make

---

* Reprinted by permission of Walter Shulits, Cadet, U. S. Military Academy West Point, New York.

his life far more enjoyable and productive. It is as Jean Jacques Rousseau states in *The Social Contract:* ". . . and even the most prudent judged it not inexpedient to sacrifice one part of their freedom to ensure the rest; as a wounded man has his arm cut off to save the rest of his body."

Similarly, along with our constitutional rights and governmental services, we all have a patriotic obligation to serve our country in any capacity in which we are capable. To me, it seems odd that the individual who burns his draft card will at the same time accept the recreational facilities, police and fire protection, and communications media which his governed society provides. It is also ironic that this same individual will use every legal trick in the book to avoid a prison sentence. Can a person accept one part of a society while rejecting the other? And if everyone "takes" without "giving," will not anarchy soon destroy our society?

Thus, while a young man may violently oppose our Vietnam policy, it is his patriotic duty to serve if called upon. And one thing must be remembered—a true patriot fights not only the visible forces of communism, fascism, and tyranny, but also the unseen force called anarchy.

What Do You Think?

1. Do *you* think "it is odd that the individual who burns his draft card will at the same time accept the recreational facilities, police and fire protection, and communications media which his governed society provides"?

2. The writer asks what seems to be a rhetorical question (a question that implies its own answer): "Can a person accept one part of society while rejecting the other?" Does this seem like a sound argument in favor of military service for all? Explain your answer.

Why I Am in the Army *

Two reasons for my enlisting in the United States Army were that I wanted to travel and to have some voice in the nature of my military training. Had I been drafted, my choices would probably have been limited.

In the "New Action Army" the jobs available to the soldier are far more varied than they were in the World War II period. With electronics and communications playing such a large part in warfare today, these

---

* Reprinted by permission of SP/4 William A. Butz, second-term enlistee on duty in Vietnam.

two fields alone offer hundreds of different and interesting jobs. There are also many other areas of opportunity, such as aircraft operation and maintenance, intelligence, supply, and administration. All these M.O.S. (military occupational specialty) fields frequently lead to a lifetime career, either in or out of the service.

My major reason for enlisting, however, was restlessness, a problem bothering many young men and women. At 19, just out of high school and going to college merely to please society, I, like many others in this position, found the social side of college attractive but the academic chores dull and tiresome. I just couldn't face four more years of school before I had had a chance to see something of the world.

Some say that military service is an easy way of escaping from the need to prepare for the future or that such service interferes with one's future. I do not agree; I look on my service time as a temporary postponement of plans and as chance to see what really interests me. Three, four, even six years do not represent a great amount of time when one considers the experience that a serviceman receives during his tour of duty. After four years in the service, I will be 23, not too old to begin college or to enter some other occupation. And in the meantime I will have lived in a number of different areas of the world and seen more than most 23-year-old college graduates may ever see. If I should go on to college after I am discharged, the dull European history course will come to life because I will have seen first-hand many of the areas of the world that are studied. This will probably make me a more interested, if not a better, student of history than my classmates.

But perhaps I won't be going to college. If not, the training that I have received in the Army may lead to a civilian job related to my M.O.S., with time in service counting toward seniority and retirement. Actually, then, my service time is not "wasted" or an easy way out of assuming responsibility, but a preparation for civilian life.

Because of the nature of modern armed forces, the individual serviceman must be able to bear more responsibility and be specialized in his duties. The enlisted man may "lose" three to six years, but he will be trained for a specific field which is suited to his aptitude. I have not only become aware of some of my talents, but I have received training in these areas and am considering them as a possible basis for a career, or at least as an avocation.

Many young men and women join the armed forces purely out of a sense of patriotic duty. Perhaps all enlistees do so, either consciously or subconsciously. I cannot honestly claim that I enlisted purely out of a sense of loyalty to the United States. However, I have always been aware of the importance of preserving the ideals of democracy, not only in this country but throughout the world. Coming into direct contact with the threat of communism, not only among our allies but among our enemies, has given me a clearer understanding of the importance of our military effort. I may not be any more patriotic or more devoted to the ideals of democracy than I was before I enlisted, but I have a clearer and broader perspective, which should make me a better citizen and a more intelligent voter.

I would recommend enlistment in the armed forces to any young man or woman who, after high school, is "hung up," uncertain about his future. Young men of 18 and over have an obligation to their country, an important obligation. Discharging that obligation can be for them, as it was for me, an interesting and satisfying experience.

What Do You Think?

1.   Do you think that the writer is representative of a considerable number of young men in the United States today, or is his position an exceptional one? Explain.

2.   Do you think that, at least for some young men, it would be beneficial to discharge their service obligations before entering college or beginning some other occupational training? Explain your answer.

ACTIVITIES FOR INVOLVEMENT

1.   After considering the various opinions expressed in this chapter concerning patriotism, write your own definition of "A Patriot."

2.   Invite the local recruiting officer to speak to your class on the topic "What Opportunities Does the Army [or some other branch of the armed forces] Offer to a Young Man?"

3.   Invite a member, perhaps an official, of the American Legion or the Veterans of Foreign Wars, to speak to your class about the duty of a citizen to serve in the armed forces.

4.   Select a team composed of five or six members of your class to interview men who have made a career of the Army or some other branch of the armed forces. The class can suggest a limited number of questions which the interviewers will ask. For example, "Why did you decide to make a career of military service?" "What would you say are the most important advantages and benefits to be derived from such a career?" "Would you select the same career if you had to do it over again?"

5.   If you have a relative, perhaps a father, who has served or is serving in the armed forces as a volunteer, ask him why he chose to do so.

6.   Now that you have read all the arguments in favor of military service, which one do you think is the soundest and most convincing? If you disagree with the views of any of these articles, write a reply in which you attempt to refute the arguments presented.

7.   Traditionally, many people have tried to give evidence of their patriotic feeling in various ways besides serving in the armed forces—for example, by displaying the American flag on certain holidays. What other action or symbols of patriotism have you observed and what meaning do they have?

8.   Form an interviewing team which will ask a number of veterans of World War I, World War II, the Korean War and the war in Vietnam the question: How do you feel about having had to serve in the armed forces? After the interviews have been completed, do the following:

a. Compare the interviews given by the veterans of the various wars to see whether there is any significant difference in the answers.

b. If there is a significant difference, hold a class discussion in which you try to explain the reasons for the difference.

4

Why Do Men Oppose Military Service?

"And they shall beat their swords into plowshares, and their spears into pruninghooks."

Isaiah 2:4

Why do some men oppose serving in the armed forces? Why do they choose to accept such offensive labels as "coward," "draft-dodger," and "traitor" rather than bear arms? What motivates them to put on public demonstrations, to burn their draft cards, to resort to all sorts of devices to avoid military service—even to leaving the country? What reasons are there for exempting an able-bodied man from military service? In this chapter you will find a variety of answers to these questions—religious, moral, political, and economic. The selections range from informal statements by students to classic commentaries by famous men.

1. OUT OF THE KITCHEN—INTO THE SOUP *

One of the most dramatic methods of protesting against war—and one that has caused a good deal of controversy—is the burning of draft cards. Here is an account of a young man who was among the first to burn his draft card.

When David Miller, 22, graduated from Syracuse's Jesuit-run Le Moyne College last June, he headed for New York and went to work

---

* From *Time,* November 5, 1965. Reprinted by permission of *Time.* Copyright Time Inc., 1965.

without pay in a Bowery-area soup kitchen run by the Catholic Worker movement, a charitable group that is also passionately pacifist. In mid-October Miller got out of the kitchen long enough to land in the soup.

Climbing atop a sound truck parked for a Manhattan rally protesting the Vietnam war, Miller announced: "I believe the napalming of villages in Vietnam is an immoral act. I hope this will be a significant political act, so here goes." Then, while cameras whirred, he set fire to his draft card (classification 1-A) with a cigarette lighter.

He was arrested three days later. Last week in federal court Miller became the first American citizen arraigned under a law, signed last Aug. 30 by President Johnson, by which anyone who burns his draft card commits a federal offense. Miller pleaded innocent, was released on $500 bond until his trial on Nov. 22. (In the meantime, he started a 30-day sentence for intruding on private property during a civil rights demonstration in Syracuse in March.) As he walked out of the courthouse after his arraignment, he declared: "Destruction of a draft card poses no greater threat to national security than the destruction of a bubble-gum card."

It should certainly prove more costly. The maximum penalty under the law is five years in prison and a $10,000 fine—which may possibly preclude draft-card burning from rivaling panty raids or telephone-booth packing as a post-adolescent craze.

What Do You Think?

1. Do you agree with Miller's contention that "Destruction of a draft card poses no greater threat to national security than the destruction of a bubble-gum card"? Explain your reasoning.

2. In the last paragraph the burning of draft cards is put into the same category as other "post-adolescent" crazes, such as panty raids or telephone-booth packing. Is this a statement of fact or opinion? If the latter, is it accurate and fair? Why or why not?

2. CONSCIENTIOUS OBJECTION TO PARTICULAR WARS *

A great deal of criticism has been leveled at those who burn their draft cards or indicate their opposition to war and/or the draft in other dramatic ways. The writer of this article discusses the character and motives of these men. Are we judging them fairly?

---

* Excerpted from *The Saturday Evening Post*, February 1966. Reprinted by permission.

Few recent events in this country have provoked such widespread and vociferous indignation as the refusal of a few young Americans to be drafted for combat duty in Vietnam. The first youth who publicly burned his draft card, a 22-year-old New Yorker named David Miller, was pursued and arrested in New Hampshire by a squad of FBI agents; and other young demonstrators, whose only offense was participation in sit-ins, have lost their student deferments and been speedily reclassified I-A. With almost no debate, as if under siege, Congress abruptly passed, and the President signed, a law making it a serious crime to burn a draft card.

We are rightly concerned about disrespect for the law in any shape or form. Some of these Vietnam objectors may be hypocrites, or sensation-mongers, or outright subversives, of course. But surely, for those sincere and loyal citizens who believe the war to be unjust, military service in Vietnam presents a terrible moral issue. And, I submit, we are seriously discriminating against this sincere minority and putting its members in an impossible moral position.

To demonstrate, let us say that one young man announces that he is forbidden by conscience to take part in *any* war. The legal response, and much of the public verdict, would be that he should not be required to serve in the military, and a way would be provided for him to perform other service honorably. But there are other young men who may say that World War II was just because Hitler had to be fought, but that the Spanish-American War was unjust and the Vietnamese War is unjust and therefore they cannot conscientiously support it. Like John Quincy Adams, who fought for the American Revolution but bitterly opposed the Mexican War, they are willing to participate in "just" wars but not an "unjust" one. Public opinion denounces them, and the law says they can be sent to a federal penitentiary. . . .

Congress has never faced the fact that just as one may oppose *all* war on religious grounds without being a Quaker or a Mennonite, one may oppose a single war—for instance, Vietnam—on religious or ethical grounds without being a total pacifist.

Many will say that a citizen has no more right to refuse to fight than to refuse to obey other laws. And if one does have such a right, may he not also refuse to pay taxes to support the "unjust war"? In time of national emergency, it will be argued, the opposition of a minority to an essential law may deprive the nation of its very right to survive. The proper route of protest, the argument continues, is through the courts or legislation, not by civil disobedience.

From the point of view of the sincere objector himself, there is only one answer to these arguments, and it is not really an answer at all, but rather the response that Martin Luther made to similar entreaties: "Here I stand; I cannot do otherwise."

For every man there can be some things which conscience forbids, even while the law says, "You must!" Rarely will a command of the State and one's ethical standards clash so violently, but when they do, a man must give priority to his own deepest convictions or lose respect for his own moral worth. . . .

Henry Thoreau said it even more briefly: "I think that we should be men first, and subjects afterward."

It has been our pride in America to produce men, not just subjects, and to accommodate our laws, where possible, to the demands of the individual conscience. This is often an excruciating task, and many times, on such issues as fluoridation and vaccination, the moral issues have been found insufficient and the conscience has been obliged to give way. But plainly the law can and should make exception for those who wish to serve in other ways than by carrying a gun in a particular war. We can and should recognize what our existing conscientious-objector laws imply—that the draft makes a unique demand upon the citizen.

The soldier cannot later work for "repeal" of war he believes unjust and for resurrection of the enemy; in time of war we do ask our citizens to commit the one act which all religions otherwise recognize to be, *prima facie,* a moral sin—killing. Surely if the problem were confronted squarely, few of us would want our citizens to suspend moral judgment in wartime. When a man is asked to kill in the service of his country, we should not ask him to say to himself as he pulls the trigger: "I am not responsible for this act; I am just a tool of national policy; I am justified because I am acting under superior orders."

Morally speaking, the conscientious objector may feel that his right not to fight is absolute, but in the political realm (as the Supreme Court has held time and time again) there are few if any, absolute rights; and when an intransigent minority threatens the majority's right to govern, the minority must admittedly give way. But by the same token the majority have no right to *assume* that permitting dissenters to live as their consciences dictate will tear society apart. It is this kind of assumption— "Give 'em an inch and they'll take a foot"—which has been responsible for some of the most murderous repressions of minorities in history. What I plead for is a new, pragmatic approach to the problem.

My proposal is a simple one. Force a real, hard choice on the zealots. Expand our conscientious-objector statute so that those who are "conscientiously opposed" to a particular war can preserve their consciences without becoming criminals. The present law says that pacifists shall be assigned "to noncombatant service" or to "civilian work contributing to the maintenance of the national health, safety or interest." To this I would add a new classification for the particular-war objector. He, too, would be called into service for the national interest. If it were killing in Vietnam to which he conscientiously objected, he could go into noncombatant service there—as the conscientious objectors may do now. If, in good conscience, he couldn't take part in the Vietnam war at all, then he could do combat duty on another front, perhaps Korea or Germany. If he still proved recalcitrant, he could be treated much like a general conscientious objector, and be posted to difficult or hazardous civilian work, perhaps in the Southwest deserts or the swamps of Central Africa —wherever he was needed. If administering this plan sounds like an unbearable burden, one must reply that this is the kind of price we pay, and pay again, to protect the rights of suspected criminals and even reckless drivers. . . .

The vast majority of America's young men have always been conformist in useful ways. They prefer to go where the action is—to be with their colleagues, even in war, rather than be banished from their company. And as Vietnam demonstrates daily, Americans make willing, brave and skillful soldiers.

Defense Department officials would probably be the first to admit that if an announcement were made tomorrow at Danang Air Base offering to transfer out any man who had lost faith in the American cause and who was prepared to explain his views to a hearing board, there would be few—if any—takers. In recent years the U. S. Army has permitted servicemen who are suddenly "converted" to total conscientious objection to leave the service without dishonor. Very few have tried to use this policy as a means of avoiding service. . . .

Few young men would or could achieve the new status of the conscientious objector to the particular war. Not only would it put their convictions to the test, but it could bring them some duty as hazardous and dirty as combat. Nevertheless, there are such men among us today, and at present they are ordered either to fight, contrary to their beliefs, or to go to jail. This situation is intolerable. Thoreau, in his Biblical way, went directly to the point: "Is there not a sort of blood shed when the conscience is wounded? Through this wound a man's real manhood and immortality flow out, and he bleeds to an everlasting death."

We cannot admit that national security and liberty of conscience are incompatible, at least not until we have made an effort to reconcile them. The objectors to particular wars should be put in their place—a place where they need not trouble their countrymen unduly, or vice versa, and also where they will not give aid and comfort to the enemy. It need not be a very pretty place, and certainly not a glamorous or an easy one. But permitting these difficult and dedicated young people to keep their consciences intact will achieve the same advantage for the rest of us. Is it not plain that one of the main reasons we are made so nervous by these few young men is that we fear we may not be giving them a fair judgment?

1.　Do you think the author provides a good defense for those who oppose war on grounds of conscience? Explain your answer.

2.　Do you think the author's plan to allow conscientious objectors "to keep their consciences intact" is practical, workable, and fair?

3.　THE MYSTERIOUS STRANGER *

The following are excerpts from The Mysterious Stranger, *by Mark Twain. The chief character of the tale is Satan, an angel and nephew of the celebrated relative of the same name. He has come to the sixteenth-century village of Eseldorf, under the assumed name "Philip Traum." In the chapter from which this selection is taken, he employs his supernatural powers to give three boys a vision of the history of mankind. His particular concern here is to show the part that violence, bloodshed, and war have played in human history.*

"Very well," he said, "would you like to see a history of the progress of the human race?—its development of that product it calls civilization?"

We [the boys] said we should.

So, with a thought, he turned the place into the Garden of Eden, and we saw Abel praying by his altar; then Cain came walking toward him with his club, and did not seem to see us, and would have stepped on my foot if I had not drawn it in. He spoke to his brother in a language we did not understand; then he grew violent and threatening, and we knew what was going to happen and turned away our heads for the moment; but we heard the crash of the blows and heard the shrieks and the groans; then there was silence and we saw Abel lying in his blood and gasping out his life, and Cain standing over him and looking down at him, vengeful and unrepentant.

Then the vision vanished and was followed by a long series of unknown wars, murders, and massacres.

*　　*　　*　　*　　*

Next came the Hebraic wars, and we saw the victors massacre the survivors and their cattle, and save the young girls alive and distribute them around.

*　　*　　*　　*　　*

Next we had Egyptian wars, Greek wars, Roman wars, hideous drenchings of the earth with blood, and we saw the treacheries of the Romans toward the Carthaginians, and the sickening spectacle of the massacre of those brave people. Also we saw Caesar invade Britain— "not that those barbarians had done him any harm, but because he wanted their land, and desired to confer the blessings of civilization upon their widows and orphans," as Satan explained.

Next Christianity was born. Then ages of Europe passed in review before us and we saw Christianity and Civilization march hand in hand through those ages, "leaving famine and death and desolation in their wake, and other signs of the progress of the human race," as Satan observed.

And always we had wars, and more wars, and still other wars— all over Europe, all over the world. "Sometimes in the private interest of royal families," Satan said, "sometimes to crush a weak nation; but never a war started by the aggressor for any clean purpose—there is no such a war in the history of the race."

"Now," said Satan," you have seen your progress down to the present, and must confess that it is wonderful—in its way. We must now exhibit the future."

He showed us slaughters more terrible in their destruction of life, more devastating in their engines of war, than any we had seen.

"You perceive," he said, "that you have made continual progress. Cain did his murder with a club; the Hebrews did their murders with javelins and swords; the Greeks and Romans added protective armor and the fine arts of military organization and generalship; the Christian has added guns and gunpowder; a few centuries from now he will have so greatly improved the deadly effectiveness of his weapons of slaughter that all men will confess that without Christian civilization war must have remained a poor and trifling thing to the end of time."

*   *   *   *   *

"It is a remarkable progress. In five or six thousand years five or six high civilizations have risen, flourished, commanded the wonder of the world, then faded out and disappeared, and not one of them except the latest ever invented any sweeping and adequate way to kill people. They all did their best—to kill being the chiefest ambition of the human race and the earliest incident in its history—but only the Christian civilization has scored a triumph to be proud of. Two or three centuries from now it will be recognized that all the competent killers are Christians; then the pagan world will go to school to the Christian—not to acquire his religion, but his guns. The Turk and the Chinaman will buy those to kill missionaries and converts with."

*   *   *   *   *

"And what does it amount to?" said Satan, with his evil chuckle. "Nothing at all. You gain nothing; you always come out where you went in. For a million years the race has gone on monotonously propagating itself and monotonously reperforming this dull nonsense—to what end? No wisdom can guess! Who gets a profit out of it? Nobody but a parcel of usurping little monarchs and nobilities who despise you; would feel defiled if you touched them; would shut the door in your face if you proposed to call; whom you slave for, die for, and are not ashamed of it but proud; whose existence is a perpetual insult to you and you are afraid to resent it."

*   *   *   *   *

"There has never been a just one [war], never an honorable one—on the part of the instigator of the war. I can see a million years ahead and this rule will never change in so many as half a dozen instances. The loud little handful—as usual—will shout for the war. The pulpit will—warily and cautiously—object—at first; the great, big, dull bulk of the nation will rub its sleepy eyes and try to make out why there should be a war and will say, earnestly and indignantly, 'It is unjust and dishonorable and there is no necessity for it.' Then the handful will shout louder. A few fair men on the other side will argue and reason against the war with speech and pen, and at first will have a hearing and be applauded, but it will not last long; those others will outshout them, and presently the anti-war audiences will thin out and lose popularity. Before long you will see this curious thing: the speakers stoned from the platform, and free speech strangled by hordes of furious men who in their secret hearts are still at one with those stoned speakers—as earlier—but do not dare to say so. And now the whole nation—pulpit and all—will take up the war-cry and shout itself hoarse, and mob any honest man who ventures to open his mouth, and presently such mouths will cease to open. Next the statesmen will invent cheap lies, putting the blame upon the nation that is attacked, and every man will be glad of those conscience-soothing falsities and will diligently study them, and refuse to examine any refutations of them, and thus he will by and by convince himself that the war is just and will thank God for the better sleep he enjoys after this process of grotesque self-deception."

What Do You Think?

1.   Can you think of any exception to the statement "There has never been a just one [war], never an honorable one—on the part of the instigator of the war"?

2.   The last paragraph is a kind of prophecy, a look into the future, with respect to war. Do you think what Twain says is an accurate picture of action and opinion in the United States today? Explain.

3.   What do you think was Twain's purpose in providing a survey of war down through history?

4. THE COST OF WAR

In the preceding selection Mark Twain writes in general terms of the wastefulness of war. You will find it interesting to examine the following statistics on what war has cost the United States in terms of lives and money.

WARS	U. S. MILITARY DEATHS	WAR COSTS
Revolutionary War	4,435	(not available)
War of 1812	2,260	133,700,000
Mexican War	1,733	166,000,000
Civil War		
Union Forces	364,511	3,000,000,000
Confederate Forces	258,000	2,000,000,000
Spanish-American War	2,446	568,700,000
World War I	116,516	25,729,000,000
World War II	405,399	399,000,000,000
Korean War	54,246	18,000,000,000 *
Vietnam Military Action		
United States Forces (Jan. 1968)	25,616	50,600,000,000
South Vietnamese Forces	69,802	(not available)
Estimated daily expenditures during fiscal year 1968		67,200,000 **
Estimated deaths among South Vietnamese civilians as a result of military action from Jan. 1964 through May 1968	11,000	

* These figures are from *The World Book Encyclopedia,* 1965 edition. The *Encyclopedia Britannica,* 1967 edition, gives the total expenditures for World War I as 32,261,000,000, and the estimated costs of World War II as 387,000,-000,000.

** Statistics on Vietnam were supplied by the Office of the Assistant Secretary of Defense.

1. After studying these statistics, what conclusions, if any, do you draw concerning war in general or particular wars?
2. Do you think that the cost of war in lives and money is an entirely valid argument against all wars? Against particular wars? What would the "cost" have been if these wars had not been fought?
3. Suppose the money expended in one of our major wars, or even in just one day of military action in Vietnam, had been used for civilian purposes, what might this have meant for the United States? If you think the money might have been better spent in this way, to what use or uses do you think it should have been put?

5. WHAT IS PATRIOTISM?

In Chapter 3 you read definitions and discussions of patriotism which clearly indicated that service to one's country represented the highest form of conduct. But some serious thinkers have challenged this concept and pointed out that patriotism, in some cases, may actually be an evil. How do these famous and responsible men differ in their interpretations of the term "patriotism"?

How Patriotic Can We Get? *

It is very difficult to extract any uniform definition of patriotism from the writings of the great authors. Although all would probably agree that patriotism is in some way connected with love of one's country, they disagree about the nature of the action, if any, that should follow from patriotic sentiments. In addition, many of the great writers reject the notion that patriotism is valuable and they urge that it ought to be discouraged.

Disagreement also exists concerning the balance that should be struck when the obligations of patriotism are opposed to the demands of other loyalties or to the demands of conscience.

Patriotism is a difficult subject to discuss because it is a subject steeped in emotion. Patriotism is often thought to be genuine only if an

---

* By Mortimer Adler, Sunday *Patriot-News,* February 18, 1968. Reprinted with permission of Mortimer Adler and Publishers-Hall Syndicate.

individual is committed to both the welfare and the policies of his country without qualification. There are, for example, individuals who deem it unpatriotic to question the wisdom or virtue of particular governmental policies—such as the conflict in Vietnam. These individuals view any attempt to criticize either the conduct of the war, the rightness of the war, or the necessity of the war, as disloyal.

Perhaps the most famous statement of the above position was the famous toast of Stephen Decatur. "Our country," Decatur said, "in her intercourse with foreign nations may she always be in the right; but our country right or wrong." Even those writers who consider themselves to be ardent patriots have rejected this absolute belief in the overwhelming primacy of nationalistic feeling.

"The man who prefers his country before any other duty," Lord Acton wrote, "shows the same spirit as the man who surrenders every right to the state. They both deny that right is superior to authority."

The type of patriotism advocated by Decatur is generally termed "chauvinism," after Nicolas Chauvin, a sergeant in Napoleon's army and an extravagant patriot. Chauvinism is generally an emotional and unreflective attitude. However, it is often based upon the conviction that one country is especially favored by God, or that it is the embodiment of a higher stage of history, or that it is the representative of a higher morality.

Yet affection and love for one's country do not necessarily rest upon the belief that one's own country always takes precedence over other nations.

The great thinkers often disagree concerning the desirability of patriotism. Rousseau, a strong advocate of patriotic sentiment, argued that "it is certain that the greatest miracles of virtue have been produced by patriotism . . . the most heroic of all passions."

Adlai Stevenson, another proponent of the value of patriotic sentiment, argued a more moderate approach. "I venture to suggest," he said, "that patriotism is not a short and frenzied outburst of emotion, but the tranquil and steady dedication of a lifetime."

Tolstoy, on the other hand, argued for the opposite point of view. "It would . . . seem obvious," he remarked, "that patriotism as a feeling is a bad and harmful feeling, and as a doctrine is a stupid doctrine. For it is clear that if each people and each State considers itself the best of peoples and States, they all dwell in a gross and harmful delusion."

And Thorstein Veblen [1] clearly expressed his objections to patriotism when he noted that "into the cultural and technological system of the modern world, the patriotic spirit fits like dust in the eyes and sand in the

---

[1] American sociologist and economist (1857–1929), popularly known for his *The Theory of the Leisure Class* (1899).

bearings. Its net contribution to the outcome is obscuration, distrust, and retardation at every point where it touches the fortunes of mankind.

"It is scarcely an exaggeration to say," he continued, "that no other consideration is allowed in abatement of the claims of patriotic loyalty, and that such loyalty will be allowed to cover any multitude of sins."

What Do You Think?

Can you think of any circumstances in which certain patriotic attitudes or actions might be considered dangerous or evil? Explain.

Rise and Decline*

For centuries, countless thinkers have denounced patriotic pride for one of its unhappiest effects: the irrational hatred that one people aims at a "lesser" people. Arnold Toynbee attributes the death of Greco-Roman civilization to patriotic wars between city states—and failure to establish international law. Early Christians rejected patriotism on the ground that man's obligations are to God, and after that to all humanity. A Jesuit general once called patriotism "the most certain death of Christian love." There is no question that chauvinism—hyperpatriotism—can be induced in any country, including a democracy, where truth may be a poor competitor in the marketplace of ideas. . . .

At a time when nationalism is growing in many parts of the world, the visible, audible evidence suggests that U. S. patriotism has taken a different turn and declined. One pointed comparison: in 1942, despite segregation, Joe Louis happily served because "what's wrong with my country ain't nothing Hitler can fix;" in 1967, despite great progress toward desegregation, Cassius Clay refuses to serve because "I don't have no quarrel with those Viet Congs."

Roman Catholic Bishop Fulton Sheen sees patriotism as "essentially linked with love of parents, neighbor and of God." Since these relationships, he feels, have deteriorated, so has patriotism. Episcopal Bishop James Pike, who defines patriotism as "loyalty to law and order and support of the positive purposes of the Government that makes possible one's freedom," finds no evidence of decline. He sees only change, toward increased exercise of individual conscience and greater "moral sensitivity."

---

* Excerpted from "Rise and Decline," *Time* essay, November 10, 1967. Reprinted with the permission of *Time*. Copyright Time, Inc., 1967.

Others, in different terms and with their own degree of subjectivity, assay contemporary patriotism in even sharper contrast. Historian Henry Steele Commager thinks the dissenters of 1967 are the real patriots. "Those who have the most affection for the country," he says, "are those who are most alienated from its present policies. Those who are not affectionate are those who are selling out the cities and failing to educate the poor. I don't think it shows any love for country to be spending all our money on bombs and ignoring the rest of our problems." At the other pole is the view of Oren Lee Staley, of Corning, Iowa, a dissenter in his own right as head of the National Farmers Organization, which does not hesitate to protest U. S. farm policies. Speaking for country people, Staley says: "Although they do not understand all that is involved in Viet Nam, they do understand one thing. We as a nation have a commitment. They support the country because of their heritage. They want to see protected what they are part of and the heritage they are proud of."

What Do You Think?

1. Do you agree with the writer that "patriotism has taken a different turn and declined"? If you do, why do you think this has occurred?
2. Henry Steele Commager says that "the dissenters of 1967 are the real patriots." What do you suppose he means by this? Would you agree with his opinion? Why or why not?

6.   CIVIL DISOBEDIENCE *

What should or can a man do when his sense of what is moral and right comes into conflict with some action or law of his country? Henry D. Thoreau, in the famous essay (written in 1849) from which the following excerpts are taken, advocates civil disobedience in the form of passive resistance—terms which are frequently in the news today.

I heartily accept the motto, "That government is best which governs least;" and I should like to see it acted up to more rapidly and systematically. Carried out, it finally amounts to this, which also I believe— "That government is best which governs not at all;" and when men are prepared for it, that will be the kind of government which they will have.

---

* Excerpted from Henry D. Thoreau *"Civil Disobedience," The Works of Thoreau,* Henry Seidel Canby, ed. Boston, Mass.: Houghton Mifflin Co., 1946.

Government is at best but an expedient; but most governments are usually, and all governments are sometimes, inexpedient. The objections which have been brought against a standing army, and they are many and weighty, and deserve to prevail, may also at last be brought against a standing government. The standing army is only an arm of the standing government. The government itself, which is only the mode which the people have chosen to execute their will, is equally liable to be abused and perverted before the people can act through it. . . .

[T]he practical reason why, when the power is once in the hands of the people, a majority are permitted, and for a long period continue, to rule is not because they are most likely to be in the right, nor because this seems fairest to the minority, but because they are physically the strongest. But a government in which the majority rule in all cases cannot be based on justice, even as far as men understand it. Can there not be a government in which majorities do not virtually decide right and wrong, but conscience?—in which majorities decide only those questions to which the rule of expediency is applicable? Must the citizen even for a moment, or in the least degree, resign his conscience to the legislator: Why has every man a conscience, then? I think that we should be men first, and subjects afterward. It is not desirable to cultivate a respect for the law, so much as for the right.

The only obligation which I have a right to assume is to do at any time what I think right. It is truly enough said, that a corporation has no conscience; but a corporation of conscientious men is a corporation *with* a conscience. Law never made men a whit more just; and, by means of their respect for it, even the well-disciplined are daily made the agents of injustice. . . .

How does it become a man to behave toward this American government today? I answer, that he cannot without disgrace be associated with it. . . .

All men recognize the right of revolution; that is, the right to refuse allegiance to, and to resist, the government, when its tyranny or its inefficiency are great and unendurable. . . .

What is the price-current of an honest man and patriot today? They hesitate, and they regret, and sometimes they petition; but they do nothing in earnest and with effect. They will wait, well disposed, for others to remedy the evil, that they may no longer have it to regret. At most, they give only a cheap vote, and a feeble countenance and God-speed, to the right, as it goes by them. There are nine hundred and ninety-nine patrons of virtue to one virtuous man. . . .

Unjust laws exist: shall we be content to obey them, or shall we endeavor to amend them, and obey them until we have succeeded, or shall we transgress them at once? Men generally, under such a government as this, think that they ought to wait until they have persuaded the majority to alter them. They think that, if they should resist, the remedy would be worse than the evil. But it is the fault of the government itself that the remedy *is* worse than the evil. *It* makes it worse. Why is it not more apt to anticipate and provide for reform? Why does it not cherish its wise minority? Why does it cry and resist before it is hurt? Why does it not encourage its citizens to be on the alert to point out its faults, and *do* better than it would have them? Why does it always crucify Christ, and excommunicate Copernicus and Luther, and pronounce Washington and Franklin rebels? . . .

I know this well, and if one thousand, if one hundred, if ten men whom I could name,—if *ten honest* men only—ay if *one* honest man, in this State of Massachusetts, *ceasing to hold slaves,* were actually to withdraw from this copartnership, and be locked up in the county jail therefore, it would be the abolition of slavery in America. For it matters not how small the beginning may seem to be: what is once well done is done forever. . . .

Under the government which imprisons any unjustly, the true place for a just man is also a prison. . . . If any think that their influence would be lost there, and their voices no longer afflict the ear of the State, that they would not be as an enemy within its walls, they do not know by how much truth is stronger than error, nor how much more eloquently and effectively he can combat injustice who has experienced a little in his own person. Cast your whole vote, not a strip of paper merely, but your whole influence. A minority is powerless while it conforms to the majority; it is not even a minority then; but it is irresistible when it clogs by its whole weight. If the alternative is to keep all just men in prison, or give up war and slavery, the State will not hesitate which to choose. If a thousand men were not to pay their taxbills this year, that would not be a violent and bloody measure, as it would be to pay them, and enable the State to commit violence and shed innocent blood. This is, in fact, the definition of a peaceable revolution, if any such is possible. If the tax-gatherer, or any other public officer, asks me as one has done, "But what shall I do?" my answer is, "If you really wish to do anything, resign your office." When the subject has refused allegiance, and the officer has resigned his office, then the revolution is accomplished. But even suppose blood should flow. Is there not a sort of blood shed when the conscience is wounded? Through this wound a man's real manhood and immortality flow out, and he bleeds to an everlasting death. I see this blood flowing now. . . .

The authority of government, even such as I am willing to submit to,—for I will cheerfully obey those who know and can do better than I, and in many things even those who neither know nor can do so well, —is still an impure one: to be strictly just, it must have the sanction and consent of the governed; it can have no pure right over my person and property but what I concede to it. The progress from an absolute to a limited monarchy, from a limited monarchy to a democracy, is a progress toward a true respect for the individual. Even the Chinese philosopher was wise enough to regard the individual as the basis of the empire. Is a democracy, such as we know it, the last improvement possible in government? Is it not possible to take a step further towards recognizing and organizing the rights of man? There will never be a really free and enlightened State until the State comes to recognize the individual as a higher and independent power, from which all its own power and authority are derived, and treats him accordingly. I please myself with imagining a State at last which can afford to be just to all men, and to treat the individual with respect as a neighbor; which even would not think it inconsistent with its own repose if a few were to live aloof from it, not meddling with it, nor embraced by it, who fulfilled all the duties of neighbors and fellow-men. A State which bore this kind of fruit, and suffered it to drop off as fast as it ripened, would prepare the way for a still more perfect and glorious State, which also I have imagined, but not yet anywhere seen.

What Do You Think?

1. What does Thoreau mean by "I think we should be men first, and subjects afterward"?

2. What do you think would happen if everyone followed Thoreau's doctrine that a man's conscience, and not the state, should decide what is right and wrong?

3. Do you think Thoreau presents a strong argument for resisting military service under certain circumstances? Explain your answer.

7. RELIGION AND MILITARY SERVICE *

What position toward military service have members of Christian churches taken? Is there any agreement, or do their views differ widely? This selection describes four major positions and a variety of minor ones.

INTRODUCTION

The decision as to military service is one that confronts every young man whether or not he has reached his eighteenth birthday. This de-

---

* Excerpted from *Your Decision About Military Service,* Council for Christian Social Action, United Church of Christ, New York, N. Y.

cision brings him face to face with many questions—problems of personal convenience and adjustment; questions of national policy, such as the fairness of the draft, the legitimacy of conscription, the validity of military defense, our general foreign policy, and the merits of the specific conflict in which we happen to be engaged at the time.

The United Church of Christ recognizes that these are important concerns. However, we do not deal with these broader questions at this time. The purpose of the present pamphlet is to set out the major alternative courses of action so as to help the individual who comes to this decision as a Christian to answer the question: Given the existing world situation and national policy, what is my responsibility and role in relation to the call for military service?

THE RANGE OF VIEWS

A wide range of positions concerning military service is found within the Christian fellowship in general, and within the United Church of Christ in particular. Although not everybody expresses his belief in precisely the same words, four positions which have been recognized either in practice or pronouncement embrace the great majority of our young men. These positions may be briefly and broadly expressed in the following statements:

Position A. As long as there is no effective, impartial machinery with recognized authority over the nations, military action by the nation state is necessary not only to defend the life and freedom of its people but also to maintain such law and order as exists. Since such action serves the divine justice, and the alternative is anarchy, citizens must defend the interests of security, law and order, by force if necessary. This may be called the position of the "conscientious combatant."

Position B. Although the majority of the nation may hold to the above position, it is the duty of the Christian to witness to God's gracious will concerning the sanctity of human life by refusing to engage in any form of military service which may involve him in killing another human being. We may call this form of conscientious objection the position of the "conscientious non-combatant."

Position C. Since war represents indiscriminate taking of life and wanton violation of persons, the Christian should witness to God's love by refusing to participate in war through any form of military service. This is the position of the total conscientious objector to all wars, although strictly speaking, the objector to combatant service (Position B) is also classified as a conscientious objector.

Position D. Support of military action in the service of justice may well be a Christian's duty under particular circumstances; under other circumstances, however, the use of armed force (as when it creates more evil than it could possibly prevent) is unjust and should be rejected by conscientious Christians. This position has come to be known as that of the "selective conscientious objector."

These views are all held in good faith by some Christians today, and are so recognized in messages and policy statements of various religious bodies, such as the General Synod of the United Church of Christ, the General Board of the National Council of Churches, and the World Council of Churches. The so-called "historic peace churches"—the Friends, the Brethren, and the Mennonites—have made conscientious objection to war in any form (Position C) normative if not obligatory. Most denominations, however, have had communicants in all four groups; . . . the law presently gives standing only to the first three positions (A, B, and C).

Other views: There is also a minority of persons within the fellowship of our church who do not fit into any of the above categories. They feel impelled to express their protest against the draft, against government policy, or against what they regard as a wholly evil war, through one or another form of draft resistance or non-cooperation. Depending upon the individual's views and circumstances, the form of protest may range from peaceful demonstration, refusal to register, or the return of a draft card, to obstruction of military personnel and civilian officials, sabotage, or violence aimed at overthrowing the entire system.

Some of these forms of protest obviously go far beyond the normal definition of conscientious objection. As an institution the church does not necessarily sanction or condone any of these specific acts. . . . Recognizing that various individuals draw the line at different places, we may designate this point of view as that of the "draft resister."

What Do You Think?

1. Which of the four major positions, if any, do you favor and why?

2. Should the government give standing—that is, grant special consideration—to Position D as well as to Positions A, B, and C? Why or why not?

3. Is a conscientious noncombatant actually serving the cause of peace and serving friend and foe impartially even when he only assumes such noncombatant duties as serving in the medical corps?

4. Do you think it is fair to excuse some people from military service because of demonstrated religious belief and at the same time draft others who cannot claim exemption on religious grounds but who sincerely oppose military service on moral grounds?

8. POLITICS OF VIOLENCE AND INDIVIDUAL CHOICE *

What reasons do young men have for opposing war or for refusing to serve in the armed forces—outside of cowardice and purely selfish motives? Here is one answer to this question.

In every can of tennis balls there are three of them, which we do not think of as first, second, and third. Suppose one of them is lost: which one? We don't know: never thought of it that way. Just one of them.

In the same way numbers of men and groups of men are concepts that obscure the individuality of those composing them. In wars we hear of casualty figures and attempt to determine victory by balancing a score-card of the dead: how completely unreal it is. We have no idea of the individual experiences of pain, horror, despair, and death that are in those figures alone, leaving aside the affliction that spreads from every death like ripples from a stone: wives, children, lovers, parents, friends. We could not bear to conceive of it, and we never have to. Our culture has built up in us an ingrained defense—the ability to believe secretly that death itself is unreal. This is the lesson of every childhood game in which the slain, after dying picturesquely, jump up shouting and continue to fight; of every violent TV show and movie in which we know the actors aren't really dead: of every facile book where death avoids the hero and wipes out the man who "deserved it all along." And simultaneously as we misconceive death, we see killing as the means of settling things, the ultimate self-expression. We sure are glad when the Marines finally wipe those ———— out.

But more potent than all this in our minds today is the sense that gigantic forces, on a historic and national scale, are motivating the wars and hostility which make up our present world-picture. It is certainly easiest to believe this, because this idea frees us of choice and responsibility. Nevertheless, nations, alliances, armies, and the group of people who are draft-eligible American males are all made up of individuals, who need surrender their power to make moral decisions only if they themselves decide to. I do not think that we are aware of this in America today, but it is true, as it will always be, that every man is in control of his mind, speech, and action, and does not have to submit automatically to coercion to do what he believes is wrong.

---

* Written especially for this book by Mr. Lowry Pei, graduate student at Stanford University.

And how many people believe that it is right that the youth of this country should have a state-decreed "obligation" to make killing their business for two years, before going on to be (we of course expect) peaceable, law-abiding citizens? How many believe it is right for men to be told that killing is laudable if you simply kill the right man? How many believe in involuntary servitude (draft)? How many in regimentation, denial of individuality, indoctrination in limited and inaccurate ideas designed to increase hostility between nations? How many think the best use of America's young men in their prime is to make them into a machine of aggression with which old men can threaten the rest of the world?

How do we treat a murderer in civil life?

Is there any difference?

There are, we know, very many who separate killing in war, or the potential killing that is fostered in armies, from their usual code of morality. But there is a growing number, particularly in this generation, who refuse to be blind to the horror of killing, who refuse to abdicate their responsibility of individual moral choice. They are on the side of life. They recognize that to meet violence with violence is to add to an existing evil, that destruction will never lead to agreement, and that the oppression of individuals in an inhuman military system will lead to a debased and inhuman society. The youth of America who face the draft have begun at last to realize that their lives and decision—particularly *this* decision—are their own.

It is the responsibility of every generation to discover America again; to make its pilgrimage to it, to settle it and finally to build and create it. America is now a New World as it was in 1492, and we have before us a new image and a very old one. We as diverse peoples have been taught by religions from Buddha to Christ and as Americans by all the ideals that we were brought up with, and it should not be strange that we wish to put them into practice. This generation is trying to carry out a vision of a world in which the principle of invidious supremacy is renounced. We can conceive, as men have in all eras, of a world in which men are free because they do not need to be coerced into cooperation. And so we see young men in our time able to step outside the channeling of a warlike society and face the coercion and punishments that society offers, for the sake of a moral imperative to realize a different sort of life. This vision of a politics of peace and a free society need not stem from religion (though of course it can); it is a moral idea that is becoming clear to people everywhere. The ideal can never be met fully, but we must stand up now for our beliefs lest the world be put out before we have our short chance to make it better.

What Do You Think?

1. The writer implies the question, "Is it possible to make a distinction between killing in war and murder—to call one more or less moral than the other?" How would you reply to this question?

2. What does the writer see as the responsibility and purpose of his generation? What kind of a society would the United States be if his vision were realized?

9. A PACIFIST'S VIEWS *

I am a pacifist. On the basis of my religious training, beliefs, and personal moral code, I feel that there is no justification for taking the life of another human being. Therefore I also feel that I cannot serve in the armed forces in any capacity since I might be called upon to commit or aid in the commission of what I hold to be inexcusable murder.

As a pacifist, I favor major reforms in our present draft system, for to end war we must first hinder the government's ability to wage war: we must abolish conscription. Any government that can legally conscript an army will certainly do so. Any government with an army will tend to make it as large as possible, and invariably the temptation of having a large army is to use it.

Since no one man or any group of men has the divine attributes necessary to make a life-or-death decision for even one other individual, let alone a legion of men, I believe we should make it unnecessary for our government to have to make such a judgment.

If the administration did not have the power to conscript, it would have to rely on volunteers to staff its military. While there might not be many of these (in comparison with the size of our present armed services), there would undoubtedly be enough to man this country's defenses (until such time as the other governments of the world are prepared to disarm) but not enough to enable the administration to engage in any of those imperialistic or meddlesome ventures that lead directly to war.

Finally, as an alternative to the present Selective Service System, I offer the Community Service System. In this theory, the desired goal would be service to the community rather than martial participation. Every person in the community would be asked to devote some period

* Written especially for this book by Mr. Robert Weber, first year student at the University of Wisconsin.

of time, at any point in the person's life, to work which would benefit the society. A locally elected board could be set up to decide what jobs would fulfill this requirement and also to completely defer those individuals who had already served society through their occupations, etc. I believe this system would be more agreeable to people, and certainly more humanitarian, than our present one.

What Do You Think?

1. Do you find the second paragraph of this statement logical and convincing? Can you think of evidence that will either support or refute the writer's generalizations?
2. What does the writer imply in the fourth paragraph concerning the reasons for war? Do you agree with his thinking?
3. What do you think of the proposal for a Community Service System? Is this sort of plan practical and worthwhile, or is it too idealistic to be feasible? Explain your reasoning.

ACTIVITIES FOR INVOLVEMENT

1. Invite people representing various religious faiths to speak to your class concerning their views on conscientious objection. The greater the variety of views represented, the more valuable this experience will be. You should therefore make an effort to secure the services not only of the major churches—Protestant, Catholic, Jewish—but of the Society of Friends, Jehovah's Witnesses, etc. The speakers do not necessarily have to be clergymen.

2. Using an opaque projector, show a reproduction of Picasso's masterpiece "Guernica." After the class has had an opportunity to study the painting carefully, have a member of the class or the teacher explain the artist's concept of war as it is symbolically portrayed in this work. (Perhaps some member of the Art Department will either refer you to helpful sources of information or agree to discuss the picture.)

Some members of the class may possibly want to try their hand at expressing their concept of war by means of a drawing or painting.

3. Make a collection of recordings of ballads having to do with war or military service by such folk singers as Joan Baez. After listening to the recordings, hold an open discussion of the attitudes and ideas reflected in the ballads.

4. With the help of your teacher and/or librarian, make a list of well-known works of fiction and poetry having to do with war or military service. Various members of the class will then select specific works which they will read and make an oral report to the class on the ideas and merits of the work.

Some of you may be interested in expressing your ideas in the form of a poem, a short story, a one-act play, or an essay.

5.   Prepare a bulletin-board display of photographs and cartoons having to do with antiwar demonstrations, draft-card burning, or other incidents related to opposition to military service or the draft.

6.   The issue of draft-card burning has been one of the most sensational aspects of demonstrations against war and military conscription. Recently the Supreme Court upheld the law against draft-card burning and thus cleared the way for legal punishment of such action. Write an essay on "Draft-Card Burning" in which you describe in specific terms some of the people who have been engaged in this action, the punishments, if any, they received and the negative as well as the positive argument on the matter handed down by the Supreme Court.

7.   Prepare a chart in which you list in two columns the arguments for and against military service presented in this chapter and in Chapter 3. Then hold a class discussion on which arguments, *on each side,* are most powerful, and why. Which arguments most successfully refute the other side's position? Why?

5

Is the Draft Fair and Efficient?

Beat! beat! drums—blow! bugles! blow!
Over the traffic of cities—over the rumble of wheels in the streets;
Are beds prepared for sleepers at night in the houses? no sleepers must sleep in those beds.
No bargainer's bargains by day—no brokers or speculators —would they continue?
Would the talkers be talking? would the singer attempt to sing?
Would the lawyers rise in the court to state his case before the judge?
Then rattle quicker, heavier drums—you bugles wilder blow.

From "Beat! Beat! Drums!" Walt Whitman

Few national issues have received as much attention in recent times as has the matter of conscription, or the draft. It has had both its strong defenders and its severe critics. Out of the great amount of discussion have come such basic questions as these: Is the draft necessary? Is the draft fair or does it discriminate against certain men? Is the draft really an efficient way of supplying men for the armed forces? Is the draft being administered properly by local draft boards? This chapter will give you a chance to examine the views of national figures, as well as those of students like yourself.

1. THE DRAFT 'RESISTERS' *

How do people feel about young men who resist the draft? What kind of persons are draft resisters and what reasons do they give for their action? The next article provides some answers to these questions.

Criticism of the protesters has come from every quarter, and so has agreement with many of their views and feelings. They have been denounced by church groups and applauded by individual church spokesmen. They have been attacked in a personal way by some newspapers as "bearded bums," members of an "acne alliance," who dress in a dirty and strange way. Some congressmen have charged that their demonstrations have demoralized our troops in Vietnam. Other observers, both military and civilian, recently on that scene, insist that the demonstrators have not been taken seriously by the troops and that troop morale is good. High Administration officials have stated that these rallies and marches are giving America a bad reputation abroad, yet the international response, some observers contend, has been generally positive because the demonstrations give the impressions of America being a peaceful, not aggressive country. . . .

Former President Dwight D. Eisenhower characterized the anti-war groups in a nonpolitical way. He called them "beatniks"; he deplored the fact that "the girls are just as bad—hair stringing down over their faces"; he suggested that perhaps one way to bring the young males to their senses would be for "the girls to turn their backs on boys like that." "Sloppy dress," Mr. Eisenhower said, indicates "sloppy thinking." . . .

Rep. L. Mendel Rivers (D., S. C.), chairman of the House Armed Services Committee, charged that the Americans who were protesting our war policy were "filthy buzzards and vermin," who ought to be arrested. The reaction of Sen. Richard B. Russell (D., Ga.) to the protesters was of a more complex nature and had to do with civil rights as well: ". . . I have said on the floor of the Senate that the fact that people in high places had encouraged campaigns of civil disobedience throughout this land in other cases would bring home, at other times, under other conditions, campaigns of civil disobedience that would be much more far-reaching and dangerous than those they had encouraged.

---

* Excerpted from Chandler Brossard, "The Draft 'Resisters,' " *Look*, December 28, 1965. Reprinted by the permission of the editors. Copyright 1965 by Cowles Communications, Inc.

"One sure effect of these campaigns and demonstrations will be to prolong the war in Vietnam . . . As for the young men taking part in these demonstrations, some of them are pathetic because they are being misled by wily agitators." . . .

That these demonstrators, especially those coming out against the draft, which beckons nearly all of the young men, are *ipso facto* wrong in any of their views or feelings is the opinion of many in high places. These officials feel that protests are automatically a threat to the national unity. . . .

The protesters do have their advocates, and their statements suggest much more than just a concern with the war and the draft. There is, for example, this statement from Prof. John K. Galbraith of Harvard University, former ambassador to India, that student protests against the war "are proper, good and desirable." Over 50 university professors went along with this view in a signed statement. From Sen. Gale W. McGee (D., Wyo.) a former professor, comes this comment: "As one who has vigorously defended America's tough line in Vietnam, perhaps I may be permitted to say that we must not destroy our fundamental freedoms in the name of preserving them. This we threaten to do if we ban the pickets or smear them as Communists. I am sure there must be some Communists in the ranks . . . But I deplore labeling every protest movement as Communist-inspired because of that. This smears the overwhelming majority of the protesters in a way detrimental to their free right to object, or to oppose."

Sen. Wayne Morse (D., Ore.) goes further: "The near hysteria with which these demonstrations are being met by Government officials suggests that they are anxious to tag all dissent as lawless, reckless and bordering on sedition.

"To bring the full weight of Government police power down upon a few noticeable individuals can, they hope, spread disrepute to the whole idea of dissent or objection to a policy in Vietnam that is producing not peace, but only war and the prospect of more war."

One congressman who, like some others approached by *Look* for comments, did not want to be identified, said, apropos the new law making it a Federal crime, punishable by up to five years in jail and a fine of up to $10,000, to burn a draft card: "This is a truly absurd law and punishment. It shows real rage and fear. Something like 60 days in jail or a much, much smaller fine would be more like a reasonable idea."

Some anti-resisters have accused those in "the movement," as it is sometimes called, of being semiliterates, hysterics who don't know fact from fantasy. However, here is what one senator's office had to say about them. "They are very bright and very well informed. They really know their facts. They're a hell of a lot more knowledgeable on the war situation, and politics in general, than half the people on the Hill. When they come around here, I get the terrible feeling that I haven't done my home-work well. This generation is lots more sophisticated and involved than my own. They are determined to have a hand in forging their destiny. They won't sit numbly by." . . .

Still another congressional office—which asked not to be identified, "because this is a very sensitive area, and one can risk a lot by speaking out critically"—states that: "The President seems to have a morbid fear of these kids. If he really doesn't take them seriously, why is he so dis-turbed?"

One observer had this to say about the accusation that the marchers were prolonging the war by giving the Reds false hopes of a U. S. col-lapse: "Nonsense. Everybody knows that the marchers really are not going to influence foreign policy at this point. And Ho Chi Minh is much too realistic to think America is in a state of revolt." . . .

Only two of all the groups [of protesters] have become organized on a national scale. They are the Students for a Democratic Society, based in Chicago, and the National Coordinating Committee to End the War in Vietnam, with headquarters in Madison, Wis. The SDS claims to have 80 chapters throughout the country and a dues-paying membership of about 3,000 that is gradually rising. It was the Coordinating Committee, under a 22-year-old University of Wisconsin graduate named Frank Emspak, that organized the national peace marches on October 15 and 16. The Department of Justice is reportedly investigating both organizations. These groups preach for legal conscientious objection. It is safe specula-tion that both groups, because of their student appeal and their sense of organization, will be around for some time, long after local groups, which sprang up just in connection with the war and draft problems and which do not have an overall program, have disappeared. The SDS, for example, has already launched a program of reaching high-school students and in-structing them in the various issues involved and, quite likely, in all the views and stands of what is now called "the New Left."

What do these young people believe? What are their values? It's best to let them speak for themselves. Carl Oglesby, president of the SDS, is 30 years old and a graduate of the University of Michigan. He says: "I deeply believe in my country as much as President Johnson says he does. But I want it to stop practicing things, all over the world, that are con-trary to its greatness, contrary to what Thomas Jefferson believed, con-trary to what the American Revolution was all about. I believe America has become warped by a few powerful Government people who funda-mentally do not believe in or practice the ideas upon which our country was founded. When I hear what various congressmen and others in the Government call us—beatniks, cowards, traitors—I feel pain, not anger. They do not understand us, they have not tried to understand us intelligently. I want more than anything to talk with them, to keep in touch with them. Unhappily, I feel that President Johnson is totally inaccessible.

"I think that you have to imagine that the world is flat, not round, and in the center of this great flat world there is a big volcano sticking up, and everybody in the world lives under that volcano, except the people in the United States who are living on the volcano."

Oglesby's co-resister and national secretary of SDS is a 22-year-old graduate of Swarthmore College named Paul Booth. His feelings about the cultural and political scene he puts in the following way: "The entire culture, its ideas and positions and values, needs rehabilitating, and this is what we are up to and dedicated to continue. It is a new kind of job, you could say. There is no political orientation as such behind it. No Communist manipulation, as people have charged. I think that part of the general reaction against the marches and protests is that this sort of thing is somehow against the American grain. I mean, to a public that has become so accustomed to being manipulated and directed, it is very difficult to understand a movement like ours that comes out of a spontaneous moral indignation that is not manipulated or directed by something outside it. For instance, the President feels threatened by us." . . .

An academic view of the movement is expressed by Dr. Edgar Z. Friedenberg, social scientist and professor of sociology at the University of California: "What is new is that a growing, though still a very small, proportion of American young people is becoming ashamed of compromise on issues that seem to them to be crucial, and this does impose a strain on our usual modes of political accommodation, which have come to depend on it, but the increased moral statute of the young people seems to me a more important gain.

"One fact that is often overlooked is that most of the college students who have been active in protest movements are among the better students and those in positions of intellectual leadership on their own campuses. Certainly these are not people with a record of failure and disaffection in the system. . . . They have developed unusual moral courage."

What Do You Think?

1. For what reasons do men such as Representative Mendel Rivers and Dwight Eisenhower challenge those people who criticize military conscription?

2. What does the Senator mean when he writes, "I get the terrible feeling that I haven't done my homework well," regarding the draft resisters?

3. What is the "New Left" and how is this concept connected with such organizations as the SDS and the National Coordinating Committee to End the War in Vietnam?

4.   Which of the two points of view expressed in this reading would you support? Explain.

2.   HOW FAIR IS THE DRAFT? *

Is the present Selective Service and Training Act being interpreted and enforced in a fair manner? The following selection presents some evidence to show that it is not.

The two men looked embarrassed as they stood before an artillery major at Chicago's Armed Forces Examining and Induction Station. They were young, seemingly healthy, and well-built. They held jobs, although they had done poorly in school and had dropped out as soon as they could. They had both just been declared IV-F—not suitable for induction by Selective Service.

Each man has scored below ten on a mental-qualification test that asks 100 questions dealing with arithmetic, word use, tool recognition and pattern analysis. The questions were like these:

——— It was a SMALL table. (A) Sturdy. (B) Round. (C) Cheap. (D) Little.

——— A boy buys a sandwich for 20 cents, milk for 10 cents, and pie for 15 cents. How much did he pay in all? (A) 30 cents. (B) 35 cents. (C) 45 cents. (D) 50 cents.

The two men who failed contribute to some surprisingly dismal statistics. About half of all Americans fail the draft exam. Approximately half of these 4,682,187 rejects can't pass simple mental tests; the others can't pass a physical. The IV-F's make up 2,481,589 of this number. Another 2,200,698 with lesser defects constitute a relatively new class of rejects in I-Y—not to be called unless there is a declaration of war or emergency.

I sat behind a desk at the induction station with three recently commissioned doctors—representing the Army, Navy and Air Force—and watched a fast-paced parade of nearly naked figures present themselves for inspection . . .

The human form is not necessarily divine. Despite their youth, many of the men had flabby muscles and bulging abdomens. "It's surprising, but overweight is probably the most common cause for rejection." said the Air Force doctor. "Other musculoskeletal problems—low back disorders, very flat feet, birth defects, damage from polio and injuries to

---

* Excerpted from Jack Star, "How Fair Is the Draft?" *Look,* April 19, 1966. Reprinted by permission of the editors. Copyright 1966 by Cowles Communications, Inc.

limbs and fingers—make the largest group." The armed forces don't like to publicize the evident: a 23-year-old man, six-feet tall, is rejected, for weighing over 230 pounds. So are men with track knees, bleeding hemorrhoids, varicose veins and ulcers.

"In general," said a doctor, "we reject men whose condition would interfere with their duty or whose ailments might flare up in the service." An example of the latter is psoriasis, a chronic skin disease that may linger for years, but is not always severe or even uncomfortable.

Men shorter than 5 feet and those over 6 feet 6 inches are rejected. So are those who, even with glasses, don't see well enough. Chronic bed-wetters are turned away, along with others suffering from obvious psychiatric ailments that can be confirmed. Still, there are few psychiatric rejections—except for homosexuality. . . .

The nation's 4,000-plus Selective Service boards hold the key to a man's draft status. Within five days after a youth becomes 18, he must register in person at the board nearest him. Shortly thereafter, he gets a questionnaire: his answers determine whether he goes into 1-A (available for induction) or one of 17 other classifications.

Although there are 18 million men between 18 and 35 registered with Selective Service, relatively few of them can even be considered for the draft. Only an estimated six to seven million men between 19 and 26—the usual age range for induction—haven't already been in service. Under present rules, many are not likely to be drafted.

Besides the vast number of physical and mental rejects 3,427,909 of all 18–35 registrants are in III-A, exempted because they are fathers or because of extreme hardship. The II-S college students total 1,864,203. A minority (somewhat over 220,000) are considered irreplaceable in industry (II-A) and agriculture (II-C).

I saw for myself how classifications are made at a monthly meeting of a draft board on Chicago's Southwest Side. The session began at 7 P.M. in a corner of a vast room stuffed with the files of 300,000 men registered with 34 separate boards. The five board members, who receive no salary, were confronted with a stack of 300 cases to dispose of at a meeting that lasted three hours. The clerk, a thin, grey-haired woman, had marked her recommendations with lightly penciled I-A's, II-A's and II-S's on the jackets of nearly all 300 files.

"The board members don't have to agree with her classifications," said the chief supervisor, "but they usually do. Otherwise, they'd never get done. She just observes the regulations interpreting a registrant's status." The supervisor's judgment turned out to be accurate. There were no conflicts. The board members took turns confirming the penciled notations with firm pen strokes. No uncertainty showed until the clerk brought out a half-dozen letters sent to the board for consideration.

The principal of a school asked that a gym teacher be deferred until the term ended in June. One board member didn't know if gym teachers were "essential." Another commented that it would be impossible to hire a replacement in midterm. The board voted for deferment unanimously.

An anonymous letter charged that a youth held an undeserved III-A hardship deferment. "His mother really doesn't need his support," said the letter. "She is living with a man and won't get married just so she can claim she depends on her son for help." The board members exchanged looks of distaste. Since the complaint was anonymous, they voted to ignore it.

Four young men walked in. Every applicant has a right to inspect his own draft file, to make a personal appearance and to appeal a classification. Most registrants exercise none of these rights. Only 10,000 of 7.2 million classifications and reclassifications are appealed every year.

A 21-year-old student objected to being put into I-A on two grounds. He was really a full-time student, taking 12 hours, he said, not a part-time scholar as his university registrar had certified. Furthermore, he had an ulcer, the unhappy youth declared. "You'll be marching with the rest of them if you don't straighten this out," said a board member. "Get a new letter from your school registrar and another from your doctor."

A student who had been reclassified I-A after quitting college asked for a deferment just until June. He was the sole support of his parents, he said, until his father could recover from a heart attack. After some pointed questions about his finances, he got the deferment.

During a lull in the meeting, I talked to the clerk of a board that serves a slum neighborhood. She said: "Now that the fighting in Vietnam is becoming hotter, we're getting some men who, the day before induction, marry a woman with children. There's nothing we can do but give them III-A if they bring in a marriage license and the children's birth certificates." . . .

Campus feeling about the draft heated up after Selective Service reclassified into I-A at least 13 University of Michigan students who took part last October in an anti-Vietnam sit-down at a draft board office in Ann Arbor, Mich. Defending his position, General Hershey told me:

"Congress says we have to do business. These students interfered with our business. They defied the law. They did yell, they did holler, they did stink. In only 100 square feet of office, there were 40 of them, not counting police, cameramen and three clerks."

General Hershey believes that it was Congress's intent in writing the draft law to let persons who violate it be drafted rather than pack them off to prison. He appears baffled by the long-lasting furor. "What the hell do you think the Congress created administrative agencies for, if not to enforce the law?" Hershey asks.

A House of Representatives education subcommittee disagreed with the General when it called him to explain his action. The congressmen questioned the authority of Hershey or the local boards to decide on their own, without a trial, that the law had been violated. Rep. Edith Green (D., Or.) said Hershey was "acting as a judge and jury and upholding local boards that acted as judge and jury."

The draft law states "that in a free society, the obligations and privileges of serving in the armed forces . . . should be shared generally, in accordance with a system of selection which is fair and just. . . ." This raises some questions:

Why does a draft board in Montana, which is running short of eligible I-A's, have to induct married men while there are still some boards around the country that defer married men because they have plenty of I-A's?

Why does a local board in Missouri grant an occupational deferment to a man working for a New York company, while another man filling a similar job for the same company is turned down by a draft board in Kansas?

Why do nonwhites make up 16.3 per cent of those drafted in fiscal 1965 when they constitute only about 12 per cent of the population? (The percentage of drafted nonwhites has dropped in recent months.)

Why is a college graduate 25 times more likely to get an occupational deferment than someone who has dropped out of college?

Why do nearly two-thirds of the high-school graduates end up in the service, but only half of the high-school dropouts and only two-fifths of the college graduates?

General Hershey answers: "Why does one soldier end up in Germany and another in Vietnam? Even in combat, there is no equality of sacrifice —one soldier is on the front line, and another is safe at division headquarters." . . .

The new draft-age generation, born in the population boom after World War II, is the largest in history. Youths between 18½ and 19½ now number over 1.5 million. By 1970, they will total nearly 2 million. By 1975, there will be 2.3 million.

Today, only half of the men reaching 26 have served in the armed forces. Because of the population upswing, only 42 per cent of those in this age group will have to serve in 1975, if the armed forces stay at three million. If there is a cutback to the pre-Vietnam level, hardly more than a third of them will have to serve. When that happens, the crescendo of criticism will increase. It is already getting louder in Congress. Sen. Pat McNamara (D., Mich.) got these letters recently:

· A mother in Linden, Mich., "If it is necessary to have a draft law, let all young men be included. Surely all can serve in some capacity. I feel the present system is very unfair, and I resent my boys having to serve while others give nothing."

· A man in Utica, Mich., "I was in the first World War. It is getting me down to see those rich kids go to college and the poor kids go to war."

· A mother in Detroit, whose two sons were classified I-A, "I feel especially strong about this when my country is not directly threatened by an enemy and when so many other able young men are frittering away their time on the streets and in the colleges." . . .

Both Adlai E. Stevenson and Barry M. Goldwater, when they ran for President, wanted to do away with the draft. A top Goldwater adviser, Professor Milton Friedman, a University of Chicago economist, believes that "The draft as it now operates is extremely inequitable and unnecessary. Why not just pay large enough salaries to attract the three million soldiers we need?"

Friedman, who is one of the most respected conservative economists in the nation, argues that "The right way to look at the draft is as a special kind of taxation. Draftees pay part of the tax—the difference between the salaries they are paid by the Army and salaries they could earn as civilians."

The Pentagon doesn't want an all-volunteer Army. Manpower experts say they like having the skills and aptitudes that draftees bring to the Army. "Besides," says Dr. Harold Wool, a Defense Department manpower analyst, "money isn't the answer. How much money would we have to pay a doctor, for example, if it weren't for the draft? Money can't buy the skills we need." . . .

It is easy to understand why General Hershey, who is not a humorless man, looks wistfully at a framed document on display at Selective Service headquarters. The document is entitled, "Haile Selassie's mobilization order to the Ethiopians when Mussolini began the invasion of that country in 1935." This follows:

"Everyone will now be mobilized, and all boys old enough to carry a spear will be sent to Addis Ababa. Married men will take their wives to carry food and cook. Those without wives will take any woman without a husband. Women with small babies need not go. The blind, those who cannot walk, or for any reason cannot carry a spear are exempted. Anyone found at home after the receipt of this order will be hanged."

What Do You Think?

1. What do you think of the methods used by the draft boards to determine the draft status of a young man? Can you think of better methods?

2. Why do some college students oppose the draft? Is it "right" for them to try to find loopholes in the law?

3. What do you think are some of the more obvious inequities in the Selective Service law? Explain.

3. THE DRAFT IS UNFAIR *

Is the draft really unfair? You may get some help in answering this question from the following discussion of the main criticisms leveled against the draft.

The national agony over Vietnam has not in itself produced a wave of opposition to the draft. Rather, it has served to bring out more forcefully the chronic American indisposition to compulsory military service in general, and long-standing grievances against the existing draft system in particular.

It should be noted here that, although local draft boards make 10 million to 12 million classifications and reclassifications each year, appeals for change total only about 9,000. That is, only 0.88 per cent of the classifications are challenged. But the low percentage of challenges is hardly an index to conscription's popularity. It is simply a reflection of national resignation to it. Criticism has been consistent and now is intensifying.

The main criticisms of the draft run along three lines: (1) Military conscription is undemocratic in principle. (2) The present draft laws are unfair in operation. (3) They are an inefficient means of acquiring military forces and impose hidden costs.

Let us consider these in order:

I.

The draft, many of its foes declare, is "un-American." The United States only begrudgingly resorted to it in wartime. It is a device of the "Old World," a direct infringement of individual liberties guaranteed by the Constitution, a promoter of regimentation and an obstacle to career planning and the pursuit of happiness.

These contentions, despite the historical American antipathy to conscription, are usually rejected on grounds of necessity that have been recognized since ancient times. The Bible describes a military draft in the Fourth Book of Moses (Numbers, 1–4, 46). In Colonial times men were drafted for local militias. Compulsion is not necessarily inconsonant with democratic government, and surveys show no relationship between forms of government and conscription. The Soviet Union uses conscription; so do France and Israel.

---

* Excerpted from Jack Raymond, "The Draft Is Unfair," *The New York Times Magazine,* January 2, 1966. Copyright 1966 by the New York Times Company. Reprinted with the permission of the New York Times Company and Mr. Jack Raymond.

II.

Despite its title, say critics, the Universal Military Training and Service Act is not universal. Of the estimated 10.1 million men in the 19–26 age bracket who have not seen military service, at least 5.7 million are not likely ever to see it—and the figure may be considerably higher. There are 3,226,000 men, including married fathers, classified III-A (those whose conscription would cause hardship) and 2,443,000 in IV-F (physically or mentally unfit). It would take a war of World War II proportions to affect most of these classifications.

In addition, 2,040,000 men are classified I-Y—that is, subject to call only if existing standards are lowered. Of the 2,117,000 men with student deferments, many may eventually be spared altogether, depending upon their physical condition, family and job status at the time they are summoned. Some 231,000 men have deferments as essential workers in agriculture or industry. And of the 48,000 men now registered who were married before last August, many are likely to have become fathers or to have other reasons for deferment by the time their draft boards get to them.

Thus, it is said, students with money (and brains enough to keep up with their studies) are favored, as are men who can afford to marry and raise families, while the military burden is placed on those who cannot afford college or family obligations. It is also a matter of luck whether a married man is registered at a board with many bachelors; or whether a graduate student's board decided that he rather than a married man should be drafted, or whether men with appropriate skills get defense jobs.

The system, instead of prompting youths to go into service when they are 18 or 19, keeps them guessing until they are 22 or so, when they are trying to finish college or start a career. And youths with trick knees, heart murmurs and other relatively minor ailments are exempted, although only a comparatively small number of men in uniform ever engage in unusually strenuous physical activity or engage in combat.

Furthermore, while the "spirit" of the act calls for fairness on religious, racial and political grounds, youngsters considered troublesome in a community are likely to find themselves drafted "for their own good" by unsympathetic draft boards. As General Hershey said in his defense of reclassifying antiwar demonstrators, he believes that young men who run afoul of the law should be given an opportunity to enter the armed forces rather than be prosecuted.

It is widely agreed that most of the apparent inequities are due simply to the fact that the Armed Forces cannot absorb all the men of eligible age, even with the war in Vietnam. But this aggravation will grow worse, for the post-World War II "baby crop" is upon us. . . .

Defenders of the system say it can never be "wholly fair." And they quote President Kennedy, who said, during the Berlin call-up of 1961 when reservists complained of being mobilized while draft calls remained low: "Life is unfair."

The most important consideration in any conscription system, it is argued, is not that the burden should fall equally upon all, but that all should recognize and presumably accept the conditions under which conscription is imposed. A new law could fix a different set of priorities, but it would still have to make distinctions in order to protect families against undue hardship and provide for the national interest through the maintenance of economic and educational standards.

III.

Finally, critics insist that the draft is not a satisfactory method of procuring military manpower. It brings recalcitrants into uniform, many of whom feel they are "suckers" because others their own age are spared. In addition to morale, there is the problem of turnover. In the modern military forces, even low-ranking enlisted men must be specialists who can handle complicated equipment and understand sophisticated military routines that take months to perfect. Two-year draftees quit at about the time they are beginning to be useful. In Vietnam, thousands of men each month must be returned home and replaced because their tours are up.

In answer, however, some military men insist that only through the draft can they get the higher-I-Q and better-educated recruits they need. What they lose in turnover they gain in specialists. Enough doctors and dentists, for example, could not be obtained without the draft. And insofar as morale is concerned, many professionals say that the better-educated types they get through the draft are healthier and better disciplined than the "driftwood" recruits who sometimes volunteer—but have a way of filling up Army hospitals and jails.

What Do You Think?

1. What do you think are the best arguments suggested by Mr. Raymond in criticism of the draft? Explain. Can you suggest any others?

2. What arguments are marshalled in answer to Mr. Raymond's criticism of military conscription? Can you think of any others?

3. Would it be fair to give fathers and bachelors an equal draft status?

4. Would it be fair to draft men unable to meet physical and mental standards? Defend your answer.

4. A TEST OF TIME *

Can the draft be defended as an effective, fair method of securing men for the armed forces of the United States? Lieutenant General Lewis B. Hershey, who has been Director of Selective Service since 1941, gives such a defense in the following article.

The Selective Service System is beginning a new calendar year. It looks back on more than a quarter of a century of successful operation in 2 wars and the present situation in Viet Nam. If the experience of 1917–1918 is included, there have been nearly 3 decades of effective operation by a system in which delegated responsibility has been accepted by citizens in all communities in the procurement of manpower for the Armed Forces.

This has been an unusual experience in American history. General Washington saw the Revolution drag on for years with few British troops but with even fewer continentals or state troops that he could be certain would be available for a battle let alone a campaign.

In the War of 1812, a battle won in the morning was lost in the afternoon because some of the troops decided they would defend their country only from their side of the river.

General Scott, in the Mexican War, spent months on the defensive and in great peril because several thousand of his troops decided they would exercise a questionable option of serving only 1 year when their enlistment had been for 1 year or the duration.

Commanders on both sides in the Civil War fought battles under most unfavorable conditions because large numbers of their troops were due for relief from active duty.

The Civil War demonstrated how not to operate a compulsory system. The honesty of the lottery operation was challenged and the building of an armed force by bonus, substitution, and payment of money in lieu of induction was completely discredited.

The centralization of authority in operation by the general government, a panacea now recommended, led to riots, bloodshed, and worst of all to the breakdown in the operation with the result that calls were not met.

Secretary of War Newton D. Baker, in a stroke of genius, secured the authorization by Congress of a plan that decentralized the operation,

---

* Excerpted from Lt. General Lewis B. Hershey, Director, Selective Service System, "A Test of Time," *Selective Service*, XVII, January 27, 1967, Washington, D. C.

made the Governors, so troublesome in the Civil War, partners, and delegated to the communities the responsibility and the power to participate in the operation once the national government had decided what is wanted accomplished.

The fact that unpaid men will accept the obligation of performing this duty is not understood by the citizens of any other nation. The significance of the unity of the Nation is nowhere else demonstrated by deeds as it is by the action of communities in applying national laws and regulations to meet their share in the delivery of men.

You have read, seen, and listened to the self-appointed experts who know what is done wrong, but never how to do right.

There has been criticism during the past year and a half. Has any one charged the Selective Service System with failure to make the calls? Has there been a claim that recruiting has not been supported? Waiting lists for enlistments deny this. Has our economy been endangered by induction of critical workers in essential industries? Has there been an interference by the Selective Service System in utilization of scientific, professional, and technological personnel and the training of this type of personnel? The outcry against student deferments indicates Selective Service has done the job too well. These are the reasons for which Congress created the Selective Service System.

You have understood that it was the noisy few who knew all the shortcomings of the Selective Service System in detail but had no conception of what the Selective Service System did, and suggested only proven failures or untried visionary methods for its replacement.

Yet with all your understanding, your know-how, your devotion to duty, and dedication to country, you cannot be blamed for wondering why, you, a member of the Selective Service System, must be attacked by citizens who have the privilege of dissent and attack because you give your time to provide men for our Armed Forces.[1]

Men are serving all over the world, often with great sacrifice, even of life, that America may survive and that all citizens, including the critics, may enjoy life, liberty, and the pursuit of happiness.

Much has been said of the volunteer system as a substitute for the present Selective Service System. There is an implied assumption that the volunteer system is fair. How well I know that the volunteers, themselves, have no illusions that it is; the volunteer system depends on the poor and the willing. Far greater numbers from other classes enter the Armed Forces under Selective Service. In 30 years in the Army, I never saw a college student and few high school students except during a war and compulsion. . . .

---

[1] This paragraph is directed at members of draft boards.

Let us remember that any less than all means selection, which is always difficult, but, under our system, practical and effective. Our knowledge exceeds blind chance.

Finally, we have a system that procures men without which there can be no Armed Forces, and ultimately no survival, national or individual. Fortunately, it is a system that by its decentralization and by delegation permits our people in the communities to be a part of the process of their Government. What is required comes from the national level but, with certain limitations, they may use their knowledge and their judgment as to how the requirement can be best solved in their communities.

The fact that it works, is a far better barometer of its acceptance by the majority of our citizens, than any possible poll or study.

It is one of the keystones of our democratic forms of Government because it provides the basic means of our survival. We cannot, dare not, lose this capacity for we are dealing with national survival.

What Do You Think?

1.   What facts does Lieutenant General Hershey use to defend the draft as a system of recruitment that works well? Do you think he provides a sound argument?

2.   Do you agree with Lieutenant General Hershey's assertion that "the volunteer system depends on the poor and the willing"? Explain.

5.   THE SYSTEM *

The test commonly applied to any plan or system of action is how well it works. How well has the Selective Service System worked? How important is the draft in the total picture of recruitment for our armed forces? These questions are discussed in the following selection.

Examining our existing Selective Service System to determine how well it has filled our requirements, we are struck by the fact that it is

---

* Excerpted from a paper, "A Military View of Selective Service," presented by Col. Samuel H. Hays, Director, Office of Military Psychology and Leadership, United States Military Academy, at the Conference on the Draft, held December 4–7, 1966, at the University of Chicago.

Recorded in Sol Tax, ed., *The Draft,* Chicago, Ill.: University of Chicago Press, 1967.

essential in maintaining the strength of our Armed Forces. Despite our very best efforts during the 1948–1949 period, we were unable to maintain the relatively modest levels authorized during that period. Further, the quality and motivation of the personnel recruited during that period were too often marginal. In an infantry batallion during that period one might find only two or three high school graduates in nearly a thousand men. Technical proficiency was not at a high level; delinquency and court-martial rates were. The costs stemming from misuse of equipment and from vehicle accidents as well as those associated with the administration of disciplinary punitive systems were proportionately high. These hidden costs were multiplied many times over when the forces raised under the volunteer system were committed suddenly to Korea.

As the selective service brought in an increased volume of manpower needed for the Korean buildup, the personnel makeup of the services changed perceptibly. There was a marked increase in educational levels, skill levels, and efficiency among those brought into the service. During the months of continued high draft calls there was an increased number of volunteers who displayed many of the same characteristics as those who were drafted. However, disciplinary studies made during that period tended to show that military delinquents were more likely to be volunteers than draftees, have less education, be younger, come from backgrounds with fewer economic and social advantages, and have displayed more pre-Army delinquent behavior than draftees—factors generally related to unconcern with commonly accepted rules of behavior. A larger proportion of delinquents than draftees stated that they had planned to make the Army a career.[1]

Following the Korean War, as the draft calls declined, so too did both the number and quality of those volunteering. The numbers drafted amounted to the number required to provide sufficient incentive for the volunteers plus the number needed to fill the spaces they didn't fill. During the mid-Fifties the percentage of volunteers climbed slowly from about 60 to, in some years, over 80 per cent. However, once again the high school dropout became the typical volunteer and the frequency of delinquency with its associated human, material, and economic costs began to rise. In 1958, the Department of Defense sought and obtained authority to raise the mental and physical standards for draftees. The reasons for this move were the increasing demand for highly qualified men with the advent of new weapons, the growing surplus of eligible men in the draft "pool," and the desire to improve the effectiveness of

---

[1] George Washington University Human Resources Research Office, *A Preliminary Investigation of Delinquency in the Army,* Technical Report No. 5, April 1954, p. V–VI. See also U. S. Army Research Office, Correlates of Disciplinary Record in a Wide Range Sample, Technical Research, Note 125, August 1962.

military manpower through reducing costs incident to the administration of discipline and administrative discharges.

This increase in entrance standards brought in some dramatic changes. The Army was able to close down four out of five of its disciplinary barracks and the number it discharged for reasons other than honorable was reduced from 22 per thousand in 1957 to 16 per thousand in 1965. Noteworthy as these gains were, the most telling gains resulted from the increased proficiency and professionalization of the military units themselves. A significant result of the increase in quality input was the steady improvement in reenlistments during this period, reflecting higher morale, greater satisfaction with the service and improved primary group solidarity. . . .

Our commanders in Vietnam have been unanimous in their praise of the quality of the soldiers being provided. Even a cursory glance at our training centers today reveals ample evidence that we are producing a high quality of soldier. It is exceedingly doubtful whether we could have manned our modern air, sea, and ground units without this high quality. In terms of contributing to the efficiency of the Armed Services it would be safe to say that the Selective Service System as it stands today has successfully passed the ultimate test of battle.

In terms of relating the Armed Forces to society, the steady mixture of selective service men in the ranks and ROTC graduates among the officers has continued to maintain the integration of the military institution with society at large. As far as the services are concerned, they visualize themselves as a part of American society performing a vital service for the nation.

What Do You Think?

1. What specific evidence is presented here to show that the Selective Service System works well? Did your reading of this selection cause you to reject, or at least to reexamine, opinions you had held concerning Selective Service, volunteers, etc.? Explain.

2. In the next-to-last paragraph the writer states that the Selective Service System has "passed the ultimate test of battle." Do you agree or disagree that this is, or should be, the ultimate test of the Selective Service System? Explain.

6. A VIEW ON COMPULSORY MILITARY SERVICE *

During the course of the conflict in Vietnam, many young people have asked the question, "Should I be compelled to fight in a war which I had no part in making and with which I do not agree?" This question—which could readily arise in the event of future wars—is discussed here by a Naval officer who has served in Vietnam.

As a Naval officer currently serving a year's tour at a coastal outpost in Vietnam and just beginning my fourth year of obligated military service, I might reasonably be expected to have an opinion on the controversy over the draft in the United States. Although I am not in a position to be outspoken publicly, I do have views which I can present briefly and generally without getting into too much trouble.

The feelings of my generation—those most immediately affected by the draft—on the issue of compulsory military service are necessarily involved with our views of America's national interests. Today the war in Vietnam, which draftees will likely have to take part in, is a primary focal point of questions concerning our national interest. The draftable generation is perhaps the best informed group of young people in our country's history, and in the opinion of a large number of them, the conflict in Vietnam is not in our national interest. To them, the war is generally looked upon as the result of the failure of the policies of the generation in power. To those who share this view, compulsory military service in a war begun as a result of the failed policies of another generation, a war about which they had no say but in which they must fight, is a serious injustice.

Since I am here doing the best job I can, I obviously do not share this view of many of my contemporaries. Yet, with the exception of some highly publicized fringes, I believe the majority of those opposed to the draft under current conditions are not simply complacent shirkers. They are proud of America's past accomplishments, hopeful of her present and future promise, but impatient and disappointed in what they consider an older generation's failure to fulfill that promise in our own cities and poverty areas and in leadership for a better world. There is convincing evidence that more than any other generation, the draftable ones want to serve their nation at home and abroad in constructive ways aimed at eliminating the root causes of conflict. But they are firmly opposed to being forced to take part in the destruction caused by a war they don't believe in.

---

* Written especially for this book by Lieutenant S. H. Stryker.

Whether these people are right or wrong, I feel they deserve the opportunity to prove they can serve their country in alternative ways to compulsory military service. I would offer two different recommendations as possible ways of achieving an opportunity for alternatives:

1. Continue the current trend of bringing military pay and benefits to a level comparable to civilian vocations at similar educational and skill levels. Besides attracting higher caliber people to military careers, a corresponding increase in the number of volunteers would theoretically eliminate or reduce to a minimum the draft requirements. Thus the majority, if not all, of those conscientiously opposed to this or any war would be free to serve their country in ways of their own choosing according to their abilities.

2. A second alternative was once proposed by former Secretary of Defense McNamara. This plan called for a universal draft in which every able American would be called on to serve his country in some way for several years. The outstanding features of the plan were its complete equality, and the choice within limits of each individual as to whether he would fulfill his service obligations in the military or by working with social, economic, and educational assistance projects in our country and throughout the world.

I have ignored many of the pragmatic issues involved in the draft controversy and the basic philosophic questions involving service to the state because I feel that perhaps the most important part of the problem today is what to do with the disaffected but most valuable young people who earnestly seek an alternative to compulsory military service. Whether or not they take the form of recommendations I've offered, changes in the draft system can and must take place. No country can long afford to alienate such a considerable portion of its future leadership.

What Do You Think?

1. Does this seem to be a well-balanced, objective discussion of the problem of compulsory military service? Explain your answer.

2. What does the writer see as being the most important problem relative to the draft controversy? Do you agree or disagree with his views?

ACTIVITIES FOR INVOLVEMENT

1.   Invite a member of your local draft board, perhaps the chairman, to talk informally to your class and to answer questions. Prepare in advance a list of questions on matters that are of real importance and interest to you. For example: How does the draft board select a relatively small number of men to be drafted from the large numbers which are eligible? How does the draft board determine whether or not to grant exemption from the draft on the basis of conscientious objection? What do the various draft classifications (I-A-O, I-O, II-S, I-Y, etc.) mean?

2.   Conduct a poll to determine how the students in your school feel about the draft. Ask the following questions: (a) Do you think the Selective Service System used in the United States is a fair one? (b) If you think the system is unfair, give the reason or reasons why you think so. The results can be tabulated by using the following forms:

	% All Students	% All Boys	% All Girls
A. (First question) **Fairness**			
Yes			
No			
Don't know			
B. (Reasons for unfairness)			
College students are deferred			
Married men without children are drafted			
Draft boards around the country vary in the way they apply the draft laws			
Men over 26 are deferred			
Part-time students and night students are drafted			
The service disrupts people's lives .			
The system in general is unfair or poor			
Too easy to be deferred for physical disabilities			
Draft discriminates against younger age groups (under 21, etc.)			
Other reasons:			

3. Articles 2 and 3 in this chapter contend that the draft is unfair; Articles 4, 5, and 6 defend the draft as an effective and fair method of securing men for the armed forces. Compare these articles and answer the following questions: (a) Which side best supports its contentions by specific evidence? (b) Which side presents the most convincing argument? (c) Do any of these articles seem biased or are they all fair and objective?

4. How do you account for the sharply contrasting and contradictory opinions concerning draft resisters in Article 1? Have you heard—or overheard—people in your own community express the same kind of contradictory views toward draft resisters? You might find it interesting to jot down any remarks on this topic that you happen to hear. Or each member of the class might ask half a dozen people chosen at random the question: "How do you feel about young men who resist the draft?" The answers could then be classified under four general headings: Favorable, Unfavorable, Indefinite, or No Opinion.

5. Organize a panel discussion or a formal debate on one of these questions or on some other question formulated by the class: "Resolved: That *any one* who objects to being drafted on moral grounds should be classified as a conscientious objector whether he claims religious reasons for his stand or not."
"Resolved: That patriotic duty requires that *all* able-bodied men unquestioningly accept the draft, no matter what their religious or moral convictions or their educational or occupational status may be."

6. Recently Dr. Benjamin Spock, the Rev. William Sloane Coffin, Jr., and three other men were arrested and charged with "conspiring to counsel, aid and abet" young men to evade military service. The men were found guilty and have been sentenced to serve prison terms and to pay a fine.

By consulting newspapers and periodicals, find out the details of this case: the ideas on war and the draft expressed by these men, the reasons for their protest, the nature of the arguments for the defense, the arguments for the prosecution, etc. When you have assembled your facts, try to come to some conclusion concerning the following questions:

    a. Did these men engage in activities that clearly violate the law?

    b. Do you think these men were deprived of their right to freedom of speech as guaranteed under the First Amendment to the Constitution?

    c. Do you think the verdict was a fair one and the punishment in keeping with the nature of the violation for which they were convicted?

    d. What do you think of the contention of these men that they could not be held legally responsible for opposing a war [the war in Vietnam] that is itself illegal?

6

What Alternatives Exist?

"In any situation short of total mobilization, only some men out of many must be involuntarily inducted for military service. This one simple and overriding fact precludes the draft from being completely fair and equitable."

Mr. Edward Kennedy, Senator from Massachusetts

Because many people have found fault with the draft, various changes in the draft law have been proposed. Some people have suggested doing away with the draft entirely and substituting some other system of recruitment. Among the most common proposals have been a draft lottery, a volunteer army, universal military training, and a national service corps. This chapter will give you an opportunity to consider the arguments for and against these alternatives, as well as the opinions of high school students concerning some of the proposals. Perhaps you can think of a better plan than the ones offered here. At any rate, you should find the last article, *"Is* There an Alternative to the Draft?"*, worth thinking about.

1. THE DRAFT IS HERE TO STAY, BUT IT SHOULD BE CHANGED *

How can the manpower needs of the armed forces be met in the fairest and most efficient way? Would changes in the draft law eliminate some,

---

* Excerpted from Hanson W. Baldwin, "The Draft Is Here to Stay But It Should Be Changed," *The New York Times Magazine,* November 21, 1966. Reprinted by permission of Collins-Knowlton-Wing, Inc. Copyright 1966 by Hanson W. Baldwin.

if not all, of the objections to it, or should some other plan of recruit-
men than the draft be used? The following article discusses two pos-
sibilities: compulsory national service and possible changes in the draft
law.

Is the draft necessary? If not, what—if anything—should be substituted for it?

Between now [November, 1966] and next June 30, when the current draft law expires, a Presidential commission studying the draft, the
Pentagon, the White House and Congress must answer these questions—
and in answering them influence the future of generations still to come
of age.

National interest in the draft—more intensive because of Vietnam,
its emotional frictions and its demands for manpower than at any time
since the Korean War—will foster the public demand for change in the
draft law during the next seven months. The stakes are high; they involve nothing less than the combat effectiveness of the nation's armed
forces during a "time of troubles," and the shape of our society.

The choices are few: abolition of the draft; universal military training, national service (i.e., a kind of modern Civilian Conservation Corps);
or alterations and modifications—varying from slight to major—in the
present Selective Service Act.

Any discussion of the draft must start with the rationale for it.
Throughout its history the draft has been—and still is—intended for
one purpose and one only: to supply sufficient manpower to meet the
needs of the armed forces. If this purpose is changed, the draft will be
fundamentally changed; it will no longer be the draft.

The choices that lie ahead concerning the draft must be measured
squarely against the primary need—military manpower. What are the
needs of the military in the foreseeable future?

The Defense Department summary of its draft study presented to
Congress last June predicted a need during the next decade of a minimum armed forces strength of about 2,700,000 men—the pre-Vietnam
level. This is a conservative figure. A more realistic assessment of manpower needs in the decade to come must start with a figure of about
3,000,000 for all the armed services, a base level about 230,000 under
the current strength.

The maintenance of an armed force of 3,000,000 men will require
—if past experience is a guide—an annual average input of more than
700,000 men.

However, the population explosion has greatly increased the potential pool of military manpower; the number of men reaching 18 in
1965 was 50 per cent higher (1,720,000) than it was in 1955 (1,150,-
000). By 1974, this figure will have reached 2,120,000, an 84 per cent

increase in less than 20 years. The nation's total military age manpower pool is now about 33,000,000 men (aged 18 to 44) as compared to only 28,000,000 at the end of World War II.

These then, are the needs—the prospective requirements for military manpower in the next decade—set against the nation's human resources: armed forces of about 3,000,000 men out of a total military age population of more than 33,000,000; 700,000 young men needed each year out of 2,000,000 annually coming of age.

There is plenty of manpower; the problem is how best to recruit it, and whom to exclude. . . .

NATIONAL SERVICE

The concept of compulsory national service for all young men (and, some advocate, young women) has great idealistic appeal. This plan would require all youths reaching 18 to serve the Government (not merely to be *trained* by Government). But, unlike U.M.T. recruits, some national-service conscripts might serve in civilian jobs, a provision that appeals to those who dislike military service.

But the concept of compulsory national service carries with it— despite its idealistic and democratic purposes—overtones of totalitarianism. Regimentation on a national scale—in or out of uniform—is potentially dangerous to any democratic society, particularly one like our own in which the power of the executive branch of the Federal Government has increased so tremendously.

National service, like U.M.T., would imply the enlistment in some form of Government service or program of a great many more youths than any present program can usefully employ.

The Peace Corps has only 14,000 volunteers; all of the rest of the other high-minded, but often ineffective, Government programs—such as VISTA, the Job Corps, the Teachers Corps, etc.—can usefully employ only a fraction of the 2,000,000 men coming of age every year. More important, most of these endeavors require *trained* and mature men of judgment; high ideals are not enough. To utilize in such programs the one-third or more of the recruits who are rejected each year by the military services—many of whom are from the low-income, depressed groups which the Job Corps and similar ventures are intended to help—would be like assigning the halt to lead the blind.

National service would not be a help in remedying the present inequality of sacrifice. Any form of compulsory service which put some men into uniform and kept others in civilian clothes, which subjected some to the hazards of death or maiming, and others of the same generation to government desk jobs, would be bound to cause invidious comparisons and lowered morale.

And compulsion would destroy the idealistic concept of *volunteer* service—which is the bone and marrow of the present Peace Corps. Draft exemptions for such non-military service might well have produced the same results.

Finally, the attempt to find places, niches, for all of the youths achieving 18 each year could lead to enormous waste—even a national boondoggle. . . .

CHANGES IN THE DRAFT

. . . The chief complaints about the current draft law—outside of the basic philosophical one of the small minority who are opposed to any of those who refuse to participate in any kind of combat—are five.

(1) It is alleged that the law is inequitable and unfair in general; (2) that it fosters uncertainty in planning an education or a career since men cannot count upon any definite date of call-up, or even know with certainty whether they will be inducted; (3) that its deferment system tends to discriminate against the lower-income brackets and the non-college student; (4) that it inducts older men first instead of the younger age groups who are preferred, as the Pentagon study points out, by combat commanders; and (5) that the Department of Defense standards for enlistment and induction have tended—particularly in the years between Korea and Vietnam—to reject men with "lesser mental ability and educational attainment," thus depriving them of the training and educational opportunities the services offer.

Some of these complaints are incompatible and mutually contradictory; some are oversimplified or just plain incorrect. . . .

Nevertheless criticisms of the current law and its implementation are at least in part true. . . .

Some proposals for improving the draft law would centralize control of classification, induction and deferments in Washington, largely scrapping the present system of more than 4,000 local draft boards. These boards now have, within general guidelines laid down by the Congress and the President, a great deal of autonomy. This is one reason why X may be puzzled as to why he is inducted and his high-school chum, Y, with an almost identical background and profile—but registered with a different draft board—is deferred.

But proposals to eliminate the local draft board, or to curtail their powers too greatly, are distinctly risky. Lieut. Gen. Lewis B. Hershey, director of Selective Service for 25 years, has explained the basic reasons:

No system of compulsory service could long endure without the support of the people . . . The Selective Service System is, therefore, founded upon the grass-roots principle, in which boards made up of citizens in each community determine when registrants should be made available for military service.

The Selective Service System has experimented with various forms of data processing for the past 20-odd years. It has found that the "replacement of local boards with machines designed to digest evidence and render judgment" is not feasible. Selective Service also maintains that "most of what has been alleged to be a lack of uniformity between local-board decisions has been found, upon inquiry into confidential evidence in registrant files, to be a recognition of actual difference in circumstances of the registrants involved."

There are, however, several modifications to the draft which might improve its operation and reduce its inevitable discrimination without destroying the machinery that makes the flexible mobilization of the manpower of the country possible.

Some kind of deferment system to prevent atomic physicists, for instance, from being assigned to a rifle company, is essential, and some degree of local autonomy for draft boards to meet varying local conditions is necessary. But there are not many essential atomic physicists, aged 18, in the United States.

If the draft reversed its present procedure and inducted the young age groups first, rather than the older ones (as the Pentagon would like to have it do); and if educational deferments were eliminated or sharply curtailed, some of the objections to the present law—that it interrupts education and careers, breaks up family life and prevents adjustments to a steady job—would be eliminated or eased.

The draft boards would still face the difficult task of choosing one man for possible death, another for life. A national lottery properly applied (coupled with a more restricted and more logical system of deferments; and machinery to provide physical examinations, classification and notification of call-up or deferment a year or so in advance) would help to meet this problem.

The lottery has been sharply opposed by General Hershey and others on the basis that our present law supports to "the greatest possible degree both our armed forces and our national economy," and that a lottery would substitute chance for rational processes in the allocation of available manpower resources.

But the basis of that argument is that essential deferment classifications and exemptions and local draft-board judgments cannot be entirely replaced. They need not be. The lottery might be used, as has been suggested, after the local boards have performed their function.

If the present draft law were modified as described, youths could count upon a period of military service between high school and college. They would be examined and classified about a year before call-up; lottery numbers assigning them priorities for call-up would be drawn, and at the same time the Defense Department would announce its approximate manpower needs for the forthcoming year.

After a fixed interval—a year or 18 months, or two years—the period of "jeopardy" or liability would be ended; young men who were not called in that period would be dropped to the bottom of the manpower pool of eligibles, and could count on continuing their education and careers. They would face military service only in the event of general war or national emergency.

Such modifications to the draft law would meet all of the principal criticisms except one—that Defense Department induction standards bar the less fit. This is not a new problem; nor have the services always rejected the illiterates, the slow-witted, the emotionally unstable, even those with some physical deficiencies. The pathetic sight of the Army training grown men to read and write was a familiar one at Fort Dix and other Army posts during World War II.

The problem is the cut-off point. Some men in these categories will profit by the training they receive and will become useful to the services. Others are dead drags; they will spend more of their active duty time in prison stockades or hospitals than in useful duties. . . .

The real question is whether the services should properly be the training school for slow learners; whether, indeed, they should be used to effect educational and social reforms. This is not their purpose; the armed services exist primarily to deter war or to win it if it comes; ancillary objectives can dangerously impair the primary objective. Some officers think this already occurred; others feel that the services would have to use the lower half of the manpower pool in any general emergency and that they had therefore better learn how best to employ such men now.

The question, really, is one of degree—how deep into the less-educated, less-fit mass of our population the draft and the recruiting sergeants should dredge. . . .

Two factors clearly limit the success of any such program. One is that the sociological improvements incident to military duty must be clearly a secondary and minor mission of the services. The secondary is that such programs are much more effective in peacetime—when there is ample time for recycling slow learners and providing special training for the backward—than in times of strain such as today.

Plainly, the present program is going to do more to increase the manpower base available, even though reducing its quality, than to uplift the underprivileged.

The same comment, with variations, might be applied to the drafting of older men—a process already started. Men heretofore immune—at least since Korea—to the draft (25 and 26 and older) have been receiving substantiating physical examinations and many of them, whether married or not, "settled" in jobs or not, are now feeling the hot breath of the draft down their necks.

Given the present system of student deferments and of other exemptions, the needs of Vietnam cannot be fulfilled without drafting older men, an undesirable requirement from the military view, but a necessary one, given the present ground rules. . . .

This discussion of the problems of utilizing the nation's military manpower leads, first, to the inescapable conclusion that any new program will cost the taxpayer more money immediately. Even the suggested modifications in the draft law would add to the defense budget; a national lottery and a system of earlier classification and notification would require more employees, more clerical effort.

The second conclusion is that much more spadework needs to be done before either the Presidential commission or Congress can reasonably recommend new legislation. The Pentagon's failure, for instance, to give an adequate accounting of the savings and costs of a long-term professional volunteer force needs rectification. A detailed scenario for a national lottery system—and its effects—should be developed, published and studied.

The third and definitive conclusion is that the draft—though perhaps in modified form—will be with us for awhile. It would be unthinkable to shift the entire manpower procurement process into new and totally untried channels—least of all, in the midst of a war. It is essential that more material and psychic inducements to military professionalism be provided. In time, when the nation is experiencing a more relative degree of peace than is true today, it might even be desirable to embark —for a limited test period—on a "trial run" of an all-volunteer force.

But for today and tomorrow, the draft must stay. And tomorrow, no matter what we do, there will be other Cassius Clays, more George Hamiltons, who will cause the neighbor next door to wonder why "Johnny" was called and they were not. Clearly, what must be done is to reduce such cases to a minimum, to explain why there are seeming or actual inequities and to increase public confidence in the fairness of the draft and in its implementation.

What Do You Think?

1. The author writes that "Regimentation on a national scale—in or out of uniform—is potentially dangerous to any democratic society." Do you agree with him or not? If you do, just what are these dangers?

2. Do you think that the changes in the draft law suggested in this article would be effective in removing some of the objections to the draft? Can you suggest other changes that would make the draft more equitable and efficient?

2.   THE CASE FOR DRAFTING ALL BOYS—AND GIRLS *

Would a system of universal national service be a satisfactory method of eliminating the inequities in the draft? Here a famous American anthropologist maintains that such a plan would not only be entirely fair but would also offer advantages to both boys and girls that they might otherwise be denied.

Young Americans in every part of the land are finding their voices. Whatever the issue, more and more of them—girls as well as boys—are declaring themselves. When they speak up it is most often to protest: "It isn't fair!" . . .

It is significant that the strongest protests among young people against the present system do not come from those who have the least hope of deferment—the dropouts, the unskilled and those who have the brains but not the means to go to college or professional schools. Rather it is the students in our colleges and universities, those whom the present system most favors, who are most loudly protesting the essential unfairness of making their less-privileged age mates carry the heaviest burdens of hardship and danger. What we are seeing is not a widening rift between those who have some possibility of choice and those who have none. Instead, we are witnessing an upsurge of discontent among those most favored.

It is significant also that girls see the draft as an issue on which they too should take a stand, as they have on other contemporary issues. Together with boys, they have worked for civil rights, they have served in the Peace Corps and other voluntary organizations that allow them to give practical expression to idealism and they have joined actively in the dialogue on the issues of war and peace. All this has placed them in a different relationship to the young men of their generation even where, as in the draft, their interests and their very existence are disregarded.

The system of the draft thus brings to a head, as young people themselves see it, the question of whether it is fair to ask only a portion of a generation to give involuntary service to their country; whether it is equitable to exclude all the rest of that generation—all the girls, all the boys who lack the qualifications necessary to meet military requirements and all the boys who are exempted for reasons beyond their control.

---

* Excerpted from Dr. Margaret Mead, "The Case for Drafting All Boys—and Girls," *Redbook Magazine,* September 1966. Copyright © 1966 by McCall Corporation. Reprinted with permission of the McCall Corporation and Dr. Margaret Mead.

And all of them would benefit by the experience of a kind of life, for a limited period, in which obligation, privilege and responsibility were combined, in which no distinction was made between rights and duties as they took part in the very varied and necessary tasks of protecting, conserving and developing the country in which they expected to live as self-sustaining adults, free to make their own choices and decisions.

The current protest, "It isn't fair," has grown out of the uncertainties and inequities of segregating one ill-defined group in a whole generation. A universal national service may be the one equitable answer.

What Do You Think?

1. Do you think the government has any right—legal or moral—to require all young people to give two years of service to the country? Defend your answer.

2. Does the author make a good case for a national service corps as a measure that would have real benefit for the nation in general and for the boys and girls of eighteen in particular? Explain. Which, if any, of her proposals seem to have special merit?

3. Is there something basically distasteful about a volunteer professional Army in a democracy? Explain.

3. AN ALL-VOLUNTEER ARMY *

Could we meet our military needs by depending entirely on volunteers? Would such a voluntary army be practical and effective, or would it cost too much and perhaps present other serious problems? You will find thoughtful answers to these questions in the following article.

[N]*o system relying on compulsion can remove the basic defects of the present draft.* In current circumstances only a minority of young men are needed to man the armed forces. Short of letting men decide for themselves, there is no equitable way of determining which young man should serve and which two or three should not. . . .

The continued use of compulsion is undesirable and unnecessary. We can and should man our armed forces with volunteers. This is the method the United States has traditionally used except in major wars. The past two decades are the only exception. It is time that we brought that exception to an end.

---

* Excerpted from Milton Friedman "An All-Volunteer Army," *The New York Times Magazine,* May 14, 1967. Reprinted with the permission of Dr. Milton Friedman and *The New York Times Magazine.*

THE ADVANTAGES OF A VOLUNTARY ARMY

Even in strictly military terms, a voluntary force would be more effective. It would be manned by people who had chosen a military career, rather than partly by reluctant conscripts anxious only to serve out their term. It would have much lower turnover, freeing men for military service who are now spending their time training others or being trained. Intensive training, a higher average level of skill, the use of more and better equipment, would permit military strength to be raised while the number of men in the services was reduced. Not least of the advantages of a volunteer force is its effect on morale. Military service is now demeaned, treated as a necessary but degrading duty that men have to be dragooned into performing. A voluntary army would restore a proper sense of pride, of respect for the important, dangerous and difficult task that the armed forces perform.

The elimination of compulsion would enhance the freedom of all of us. The young would be free to decide whether to serve or not to serve. Members of draft boards would be relieved of the awful task of arbitrarily deciding how a young man shall spend several of the most important years of his life—let alone whether his life shall be risked in warfare. The tormenting and insoluble problem now posed by the conscientious objector would disappear. We could immediately dispense with investigating the innermost values and beliefs of those who claim to be conscientious objectors—a process entirely repugnant to a society of free men. . . .

Manning the armed forces with volunteers would have other real advantages for the country at large. Colleges and universities could pursue their proper educational function, freed alike from the incubus of young men—probably numbering in the hundreds of thousands—who would prefer to be at work rather than at school, but who now continue their schooling in the hope of avoiding the draft. . . .

The community would benefit from a reduction in unwise early marriages contracted at least partly under the whip of the draft, as well as from the associated decline in the birth rate. Industry and government would benefit from being able to hire young men on their merits, not their deferments. . . .

IS A VOLUNTARY ARMY FEASIBLE?

Is it not simply wishful thinking to suppose that we can abandon conscription when a hot war is raging in Vietnam, when we must maintain armed forces exceeding 3 million men in total? Men are now free to volunteer, yet the number who do so is clearly inadequate and, moreover, many volunteer only because they expect to be drafted. The number of "true" volunteers is clearly much too small to man armed forces of our present size. This undoubted fact is repeatedly cited as evidence that a voluntary army is unfeasible.

It is evidence of no such thing. It is evidence rather that we are now grossly underpaying our armed forces. The starting pay for young men who enter the armed forces is less than $45 a week—and that sum includes not only cash pay and allotments, but also the value of clothing, food, housing and other items furnished in kind. The starting pay is virtually the same now as in 1950—but prices are higher, so in terms of goods and services the man who enlists gets considerably less now than he did then. All of the pay raises since then have gone to officers and to enlisted men with longer terms of service. They have to be induced to stay in service. Fresh recruits can be conscripted—so why raise the pay?

Little wonder that volunteers are so few. Most young men can earn twice as much in civilian jobs.

To attract more volunteers, we would have to improve conditions of service. This means higher entering salaries. But it also means better housing facilities and improved amenities in other respects. The existence of conscription means that the military need pay little attention to the wants of the enlisted men—if not enough volunteer, press the button and General Hershey will raise draft calls. . . .

Money is not the only, or even the major factor young men consider in choosing their careers. Military service has many non-monetary attractions to young men—the chance to serve one's country, adventure, travel, opportunities for training, and so on. Today, these attractions are offset not only by low pay but also by the very existence of compulsion. . . .

Improved pay, better conditions of service, and imaginative personnel policies, both in attracting men and using them, could change drastically the whole image which the armed services presents to young men. The Air Force, because it has relied so heavily on "real" volunteers, perhaps comes closest to demonstrating what could be done. . . .

The question of how much more we would have to pay to attract sufficient volunteers has been scrutinized intensively in a Department of Defense study of military recruitment. Based on a variety of evidence collected in that study, Prof. Walter Oi of the University of Washington, who worked on the study, has estimated that a starting pay (again including pay in kind as well as in cash) of something like $4,000 a year —about $80 a week—would suffice. This is surely not an unreasonable level of pay. Oi estimates that the total extra payroll costs (after allowing for the savings in turnover and men employed in training) would be about $3 billion to $4 billion a year for armed forces equivalent to

2.7 million men under present methods of recruitment, and not more than $8 billion a year for armed forces equivalent to the present higher number of men (3.1 to 3.2 million).

Using the same evidence, the Defense Department has come up with estimates as high as $17.5 billion. This is an incredible figure—it would mean that the pay of every man in the armed service from the newly enlisted man to the top general could be *raised* by $6,000 a year. But even that absurd estimate is not unfeasible in the context of total Federal Government expenditures of more than $170 billion a year, and military expenditures of over $70 billion.

In any event, we do not need precise estimates of what it will take to attract enough men. Out of simple justice, we should raise the pay and improve the living conditions of enlisted men. If we did so, the number of "real" volunteers would increase, even while conscription continued. . . .

A VOLUNTARY ARMY WOULD COST LESS

The need to raise pay to attract volunteers leads many to believe that a volunteer army would cost more. The fact is that it would cost less to man the armed forces by volunteers than it now costs to man them by compulsion—*if cost is properly calculated*. The cost listed in the Federal budget might be higher—though even that is not certain. But the real cost to the community would be far lower.

The real cost of conscripting a soldier who would not voluntarily serve on present terms is not his pay and the cost of his keep. It is the amount of money for which he would be willing to serve. Compare, for example, the real cost to a star professional football player and to an unemployed worker. Both might have the same attitudes toward the army and like—or dislike—a military career equally. But because the one has so much better alternatives than the other, it would take a much higher sum to attract him. When he is forced to serve, we are in effect imposing on him a tax in kind equal in value to the difference between what it would take to attract him and the military pay he actually receives. This implicit tax in kind must be added to the explicit taxes imposed on the rest of us to get the real cost of our armed forces.

If this is done, it will be seen at once that abandoning conscription would almost surely reduce the real cost—because the armed forces would then be manned by men for whom soldiering was the best available career, and hence who would require the lowest sums of money to induce them to serve. It might raise the apparent money cost to the Government but only because it would substitute taxes in money for taxes in kind. . . .

There are some important offsets even on the level of budgetary costs. Volunteers would serve longer terms, a higher fraction would re-enlist, and they would have a higher average level of skill. The armed services would waste fewer manhours in training and being trained. Because manpower is cheap to the military, it now tends to waste it, using enlisted men for tasks badly suited to their capacities or for tasks that could be performed by civilians or machines, or eliminated entirely. Again, ask any ex G.I. for evidence.

Better pay at the time to volunteers also might lessen the political appeal of veterans' benefits that we now grant after the event. These now cost $6 billion a year or one-third as much as current annual payroll costs for the active armed forces—and they will doubtless continue to rise under present conditions.

THE RACIAL COMPOSITION OF VOLUNTEER FORCES

One objection that has been voiced against volunteer forces is that they would be staffed predominantly by Negroes because a military career would be so much more attractive than the other alternatives open to them.

There is first a question of fact. This tendency is present today in exaggerated form—the present levels of pay are *comparatively* more attractive to Negroes than the higher levels of pay for voluntary forces would be. And this shows up in a much higher rate of re-enlistment by Negroes than by whites. Yet the fraction of persons in the armed forces who are Negro is roughly the same as in the population at large. It has been estimated that even if every qualified Negro who does not now serve were to serve, whites would still constitute a substantial majority of the armed forces. And this is a wholly unrealistic possibility. . . .

Clearly, it is a good thing not a bad thing to offer better alternatives to the currently disadvantaged. The argument to the contrary rests on a political judgment: that a high ratio of Negroes in the armed services would exacerbate racial tensions at home and provide in the form of ex-soldiers a militarily trained group to foment violence. Perhaps there is something to this. My own inclination is to regard it as the reddest of red herrings. Our Government should discriminate neither in the civil nor the military services. . . .

THE FLEXIBILITY OF VOLUNTARY FORCES

Another argument that has been made against voluntary forces is that they lack flexibility—and that world conditions may change and call for larger or smaller armed forces. With conscription, draft calls can be rapidly stepped up, and conversely.

This is a real problem—but can easily be overrated. Emergencies must be met with forces in being, however they are recruited. Many months now elapse between an increase in draft calls, and the availability of additional men.

The key question is how much flexibility is required. Recruitment by voluntary means can provide considerable flexibility—at a cost. The way to do so is to make pay and conditions of service more attractive than necessary. . . .

The change in scale involved in total war is a very different matter. If the military judgment is that, in such a contingency, there would be time and reason to expand the armed forces manifold, either universal military training to provide a trained reserve force, or stand-by provisions for conscription could be justified. Both are very different from the use of conscription to man the standing army in time of peace or brush-fire wars like that in Vietnam which require recruiting only a minority of young men. . . .

ARE VOLUNTARY FORCES A POLITICAL DANGER?

A final objection that has been raised against a volunteer army is that it would endanger political freedom. There is a real danger, but it arises from the existence of large armed forces plus the industrial complex required to support them, not from the method of recruiting enlisted men. Our free institutions would certainly be safer if the conditions of the world permitted us to maintain smaller armed forces. But they are not made safer by using compulsion rather than free choice to fill the ranks.

The military coup just engineered in Greece was by an army manned by conscripts. So was the recent military takeover in Argentina. Napoleon and France rose to power at the head of conscripts. Britain and the U. S. have maintained freedom while relying primarily on volunteers; Switzerland and Sweden, while using conscription. It is hard to find any relation historically between the method of recruiting enlisted men and the political threat from the armed forces. . . .

The case for abolishing conscription and recruiting our armed forces by voluntary methods seems to me overwhelming.

We should at once raise the pay of enlisted men, improve conditions of service and stimulate more efficient use of manpower by the services. We should continue to raise the pay until the number of "true" volunteers is large enough so that the lash of compulsion can be eliminated. And to avoid procrastination by the military, who will be tempted to continue to rely on the crutch of conscription, we should set a definite termination date for conscription.

What Do You Think?

1. Do you think that the author provides sufficient evidence to prove that a volunteer army would be feasible—that it would work and not cost too much? Defend your answer.

2. Would *you* be inclined to volunteer for service in the armed forces if all the conditions recommended by the author were put into effect? Explain your answer.

4. WHAT ABOUT A LOTTERY?

One of the more recent proposals as an alternative to the draft is a process of random selection, or a lottery. After comparing the following arguments for and against such a system, try to reach some conclusion about the following: Does it have real merit? Would it do away with the most important criticisms of the draft? Is it worth trying?

Random Selection *

In any situation short of total mobilization, only some men out of many must be involuntarily inducted for military service. This one simple and overriding fact precludes the draft from being completely fair and equitable. . . .

[T]here are two compelling reasons for adopting a random selection system of determining the order of call. The first is the desire to raise the element of equity to as high a degree as possible. The second is the imperative of numbers, of choosing one man out of seven.

My bill would require that the determination of order of induction be made by random selection. I have not written into the bill itself a specific plan for a lottery, as I prefer to give the President a measure of discretion in drawing up a plan and modifying it as conditions dictate. It is my understanding that a number of alternative random selection systems have been prepared by the executive branch, although they are not available for discussion publicly.

I have in the past proposed a specific plan for a random selection system. Under this plan, the Director of Selective Service would publish each month a list of numbers corresponding to the days in the month. Thus, there would appear on the list the numbers 1 to 31 for January, 1 to 28, or 29, for February, and so on. But these numbers would be arranged in a random sequence, which had been determined by a computer or some other means. The numbers for January, in this example, might read 11, 22, 7, 18, and so forth.

The Director of Selective Service would also set monthly quotas for each State, as he does now. Each State would set quotas for each

* Excerpted from Edward Kennedy, Senator from Massachusetts, "Random Selection," *The Congressional Record*, *V*ol. 114, Washington, D. C., February 21, 1968, No. 30.

local board in the State, as it does now. These quotas are based on proportionate formulas which involve the number of qualified and eligible registrants in a specific jurisdiction related to the number of such registrants in the Nation or State as a whole.

Each local board would also have, for each month, a pool of eligible young men. These men would be either 19-year-olds or constructive 19-year-olds, as I will later explain. In a non-Vietnam situation, this pool would have seven times as many men in it as are needed to meet the quota. Under the pressures of today's Vietnam requirements, the pool might have two or three times as many men as are needed to meet the quotas.

If a local board, under this proposal, had a quota of 10 men for January, it might have 70 men eligible for induction. To choose the 10, it would refer to the list published by the Selective Service Director for January. Under this example, the first number was 11, the second 22, the third 7, and so forth. The local board selects first the man or men born on the 11th of January, next the man or men born on the 22nd, and so forth until the quota of 10 men had been reached. These 10 would then be inducted. The remaining 60 men would not be called, but would, of course, continue to remain liable in the event of a national emergency. But these 60 would not be called until the pool of men in the following month had been exhausted. Thus, once the selection for a given month had been made, those not selected could be reasonably certain of their status and make their plans accordingly.

Some local boards might face the difficulty of choosing between different men born on the same day. This apparent problem could be easily solved by arranging the letters of the alphabet in a random sequence for each month, and then choosing on the basis of the first letter of the last name.

I want to emphasize that the plan I have just outlined is intended only as an illustration of the feasibility of a random selection system. Under the actual terms of my bill, local and State quotas would be replaced by regional quotas, or by a national quota, depending upon which organizational alternative the President actually instituted. A national system would be the most equitable, and I would personally favor it.

The Case Against A Lottery *

1. *A lottery would not eliminate draft inequities.*

Any procedure which is "selective" usually causes some inequities. And as long as the military doesn't need all of the youths who turn 18

---

* From *Senior Scholastic*, September 23, 1966. Reprinted by permission from *Senior Scholastic*, © 1966 by Scholastic Magazines, Inc.

each year, some people will be called while others will miss the draft entirely—no matter what draft system is used.

As one Pentagon official put it: "Inequity is a very easy thing to talk about. But it is a fact of life. There is no more inequity in the selective service system than in the income tax system."

Advocates of a lottery seem to think that by randomizing the selection they will make it fairer. "Equality" is a catchy slogan—but equal causes don't always produce equal effects. The "cause" in this case is a draft summons. The effect varies from one individual to another—and no lottery can take into account these differences. What if a young man whose name is drawn provides his family's support? What if his being drafted would cause other hardships? The present method of reviewing individual cases by local boards, while not perfect, at least provides the best solution to these problems.

Moreover, wouldn't it be better to reform the present system without changing its fundamental nature? A Defense Department study of the draft has recommended several changes in the present system. One would reverse the order of call-up—to take 19- and 20-year-olds ahead of older men. Those who are not drafted by the end of the year would drop automatically to the bottom of the next year's list—making it highly improbable that they would ever be called. Such changes can help correct faults while keeping the best features of a time-tested system.

2. *The present "selective" system makes the best use of the nation's manpower.*

The greatest weakness of the lottery is precisely the feature its proponents stress: it does not discriminate. By choosing draftees indiscriminately, a lottery would substitute *chance* for *judgment.* The machine that picks draftees' numbers can't tell whether a man is more valuable as a student, a father, or a scientist than as a soldier.

A conscription system should be designed to channel men into tasks where they are of most use to the nation. No one would expect a business firm to do its hiring by random selection from a list of applicants. Why expect the draft system to do so?

Selective Service Director Lieut. General Lewis B. Hershey states the case this way: "I can see your armed forces when we draw a one-legged man in the first lottery and tell them here's what you get. . . . The idea that a lottery solves any of our problems is an illusion. For the most part, those urging a lottery [recognize] that you can't apply it to the disqualified, and [they] hesitate to apply it in disregard of all the other circumstances of the individual whose number is drawn." In other words, by the time you weed out the problems of a lottery you wind up with much the same system we have today.

3. *A draft lottery would be a step backward, not a step forward.*

A draft lottery has been tried three times in U. S. history, and all three times failed to win popular support. The 1863 system, based on drawings in local districts, proved so unpopular it set off violent riots in several areas. The revamped, nationwide lottery system of 1917—with a complicated system of safeguards to insure fairness—ended with a barrage of charges of fraud, manipulation, and favoritism. After three lottery drawings at the beginning of World War II, the system proved so complicated it was given up altogether. Why should the U. S. again get itself involved in a system that has thrice proved unfair and unworkable?

If Selective Service officials cannot iron out the inequities of the present system, then it should try to find a completely new system that would be both fair and workable. But from past experience, a lottery is obviously *not* the answer.

What Do You Think?

1. Which of these arguments do you think is the soundest—that is, the one that is most logical and based on the best evidence? Support your position.

2. What is meant by the "imperative of numbers" (first selection) and why is this an important factor in considering the draft lottery as an alternative?

3. Is the fact that the draft lottery has been tried three times in U. S. history and failed to win popular approval a solid argument for not trying some form of lottery again? Explain your answer.

4. Would a lottery solve the problem of who serves when there are 500,000 men available but only 250,000 are required for service?

5. THIS COUNTRY NEEDS UNIVERSAL MILITARY TRAINING *

Would universal military training be a workable, fair alternative to the draft? General Dwight D. Eisenhower presents a detailed argument in favor of such a measure.

War, of course, is always unfair to youth. Some young men have to fight and others do not, and I see no complete cure for that until the blessed day arrives when men have learned to live in peace, and there

---

* Excerpted from Dwight D. Eisenhower, *The Readers Digest,* September 1966. Reprinted with permission from the September 1966 Reader's Digest. Copyright 1966 by Dwight D. Eisenhower. Reprinted by permission of Doubleday & Company, Inc.

will no longer be need for military force. That day is not here, however, and it cannot come so long as an implacable enemy of human freedom strives to enslave the world. Today more than ever, therefore, I think that this country should adopt, as the cornerstone of its defense establishment, a workable plan of universal training—and I mean *universal,* with a minimum of really essential exemptions. . . .

THE ENDS IN VIEW

In hammering out any new system of manpower procurement and training, . . . we must keep certain objectives firmly in mind:

1. It must be a system which will provide the men we must have for our worldwide commitments.
2. It must have sufficient flexibility to permit us, in times of emergency, to bring additional men into our armed forces quickly and in substantial numbers.
3. It must, as far as possible, eliminate present unfairness.
4. It should bring to every young man an understanding of his obligation to his country and a sense of participation in its affairs.
5. It should be a builder of physical fitness, self-discipline and decent personal habits.
6. It should include the vast numbers of boys who are now exempted because of educational deficiencies or moderate physical disabilities such as trick knees, overweight problems and a host of other minor and often correctable infirmities. . . .

THE FRAMEWORK OF UMT

Under the system that I envision, every young male American, no matter what his status in life or his plans for the future, would spend 49 weeks—one year minus three weeks' vacation—in military training. Only the barest minimum of exemptions would be permitted: Obvious mental incompetents, those with some drastic physical defect, perhaps a few extreme-hardship cases.

Basically, I have always felt that 19 is about the right age to begin military service. Boys of 19 are young enough to be flexible, and in most cases they are more mature than those of 18. There are, however, other considerations. Eighteen is usually the age at which a boy finishes high school and is ready to enter college or go to work. It is a natural break in his life. If we were to enlist boys at 18 rather than 19 or any other age, it would cause less disruption in our schools and in working careers. Therefore, all things considered, I think 18 should be the age at which our young men should begin their year of UMT.

This year should be considered not only as their contribution to country but as part of their education. The government would, of course, provide sustenance, clothing and other necessaries, but the trainees would be paid only a small stipend—say five or ten dollars a month—in order to have a bit of pocket change for incidentals.

At the beginning of the year, each UMT trainee would be offered the option of enlisting immediately in our regular forces for a two-year term of duty, with all the pay, advances and benefits pertaining thereto, including later education under the G.I. bill of rights. A great many, I believe, would choose this course.

For the large number who *remained* in UMT, the year would be spent primarily in military training. It would include regular daily stints on the training base, athletics, remedial education for those who need it, building vigorous bodies and learning the wisdom of discipline, cleanliness and good personal habits. Youngsters with correctable physical weaknesses—and we have millions of them in this favored land—would benefit from good nutrition, a year of disciplined life, and special medical attention if they needed it.

The boys in UMT could and should be used in times of emergency such as floods, storms and fires. They could be useful in helping to maintain order and in assisting the victims of misfortune. On the other hand, they should not be impressed into any regular work program outside their base. We want no semblance of forced labor in America.

AFTERMATH

Almost two million boys now reach the age of 18 each year, and in times of peace or small wars we certainly could not use that many in our regular military forces. Consequently, many of our young men could complete their period of service with 49 weeks of UMT. They would then be free to go on to college or vocational school or to begin their careers without interruption—except in the case of a major war, when all our potential military manpower would be needed.

If the inducements of full pay and later education at government expense did not produce the volunteers that we need for our regular forces, then it would be necessary to draft the added men. To do this in the fairest way, we should employ the lottery. In the beginning, we would have to include in the lottery the large pool of youths who were past UMT age but were still liable to military service. This pool would diminish each year, and after five or six years would cease to exist. From then on, the lottery would apply only to the boys in UMT.

This basic plan is by no means original with me. I have merely selected what I regard as the best parts of many suggested plans and put them together in an integrated whole. It is impossible within the compass of a short article to fill in all the details. For example, how would we fit the R.O.T.C. units, the National Guard and our reserves into the UMT system? I do not believe that these worthwhile services would have to be abandoned. All such complex matters can be worked out through careful study. . . .

THE OBSTACLES

I am fully aware that the plan I suggest is not perfect. There are difficulties to be surmounted in putting it into operation.

One is that there would be some disruption of normal procedures on college campuses and in vocational schools. During the first year of UMT, these institutions would have virtually no male freshman classes; the second year, few sophomores; and so on until the end of the fourth year. After that, conditions would return to normal, the only difference being that first-year college students would average a year older—which could be a good thing.

The second obstacle—and this is a tough one—is the cost. Nobody really knows the price tag of UMT, but estimates run from three to six billion dollars a year above present military expenditures. If we wished to cut the training period to six months, costs could be sharply reduced, but I think that this would also seriously dilute the benefits. In the beginning, we would also have to build and equip many new military camps, thus increasing the early costs.

I have no ready-made plan for financing UMT. I wish only to say that a big, powerful country such as ours could surely find a way to pay the bill. Personally, I think the program is far more important than some of the public efforts on which we are now spending so much.

Still another problem is the procurement of training personnel— military instructors, teachers, doctors and so on. I do not regard this problem as unsurmountable. We could call in reserve officers for a time if needed, and I am confident that we could find the other necessary people if we had to—just as we did during World War II.

THE BENEFITS

Opposed to these obstacles are the enormous benefits that our country would reap from such a system.

First, there are the long-term military advantages. After a few years of UMT, we would have always a huge reserve of young men with sound basic military training. The R.O.T.C. would turn out better officers; the National Guard would be far more efficient. In case of a great emergency, all these men would be ready for combat after a brief refresher course, and in the event of a nuclear attack—the Lord forbid!—a disciplined body of young men in every community would be a priceless asset.

Second, although I certainly do not contend that UMT would be a cure for juvenile delinquency, I do think it could do much to stem the growing tide of irresponsible behavior and outright crime in the United States. To expose all our young men for a year to discipline and the correct attitudes of living inevitably would straighten out a lot of potential troublemakers. In this connection—although I am sure that in saying this I label myself as old-fashioned—I deplore the beatnik dress, the long, unkempt hair, the dirty necks and fingernails now affected by a minority of our boys. If UMT accomplished nothing more than to produce cleanliness and decent grooming, it might be worth the price tag—and I am not altogether jesting when I say this. To me a sloppy appearance has always indicated sloppy habits of mind.

But above and beyond these advantages of UMT is the matter of attitude toward country. If a UMT system were to become a fixture of national life, I think that resentment against military obligation would die away, that virtually every young man would take pride and satisfaction in giving a year of his life to the United States of America. After all, the good instincts lie near the surface in the young. Patriotism, a sense of duty, a feeling of obligation to country are still there. They are the noblest and the most necessary qualities of any democratic system, and I am convinced that UMT would help call them to the surface once more.

I am aware, of course, that many Congressmen regard Universal Military Training as political poison. I think they are being unduly timid. I am convinced that most Americans believe in the value of such a system, and that many others could be persuaded by an enlightened educational campaign. Most of all, I urge that we act *now*.

What Do You Think?

1. Do you find any opinions in this article that appear to be biased or that are not founded upon a reasonable amount of fact or evidence?

2. Of the various arguments for universal military training presented here, which ones do you think are the most convincing?

6.   TEEN VERDICT ON DRAFT ALTERNATIVES *

How do high school students feel about such alternatives to the draft as a national service corps or a draft lottery? Examine the results of the following nation-wide survey.

---

* From *Scholastic Teacher*, Vol. 91, No. 2, Sept. 28, 1967, edition of *Senior Scholastic. Copyright* 1967 by Scholastic Magazines, Inc. Reprinted by permission.

The vast majority—more than three quarters—of U. S. junior and senior high school students favor a "national service corps" to supplement the military draft. The program would allow young men to meet their service obligations through approved nonmilitary programs such as the Peace Corps, VISTA, Job Corps, and related programs.

This is the finding of a poll taken earlier this year [1967] by Scholastic Magazine's Institute of Student Opinion. The survey, of more than 2,700 high school students throughout the country in both public and private schools, represents a scientific cross section of all U. S. high school students.

The poll also found that only 20 per cent of today's [1967] students believe it is a good idea to replace the present draft system with a national lottery.

Asked whether they favor a national service corps, here's how the students replied:

	% All Students	% Boys	% Girls
Yes	78.7	76.0	81.0
No	18.4	22.6	14.8
No Answer	2.9	1.4	4.2

This is how they replied when asked: "It has been suggested that the military draft system be replaced by a lottery for all 18- and 19-year-old men who are physically and mentally able to serve in the armed forces. Does this sound like a good idea or a poor idea to you?"

	% All Students	% Boys	% Girls
Good Idea	20.0	21.4	18.9
Poor Idea	48.4	51.0	46.2
No Opinion	29.5	25.4	32.9
No Answer	2.1	2.2	2.0

Students answered this way when asked: "If you think the draft lottery is a poor idea, what do you think is bad about the idea of a draft lottery?"

	% All Students	% Boys	% Girls
"It would substitute chance for judgment."	52.2	51.2	53.2
"It would not provide a fair hearing for deserving individuals."	51.9	49.5	54.0
"It would be no improvement over the present system."	46.7	45.9	47.4
"It would not enable the armed forces to have the men they want."	40.8	42.2	39.5
No Answer	3.1	3.6	2.7

What Do You Think?

1.   Why do you think an "overwhelming majority" of junior and
      senior high school students indicated in this poll that they favor
      a national service corps?
2.   Which of the reasons given for rejecting the draft lottery as
      a poor idea do you think is the most valid and which is the
      least valid? Explain your answer.

7. *IS* THERE A SATISFACTORY ALTERNATIVE TO THE DRAFT?*

*Has anyone proposed a really satisfactory alternative to the draft—
one that everyone would approve, that contained no inequities, and that
worked no hardship on anyone? Consider the following answer.*

Any person who knows what is going on in the United States today
must be aware of two things: 1) There is a great deal of dissatisfaction
with the draft, as shown by the draft-evasion, the many demonstrations
against the draft, and the expressions of disapproval of the draft in our
news media. 2) Many people have earnestly tried to find a satisfactory
substitute for the draft. Leaders in public life and private citizens have
proposed such measures as lottery systems, universal military training, a
national service corps, a volunteer army, and various modifications of
the present draft law.

We can probably sympathize with many who oppose the draft, and
we must respect and admire the efforts of those who have conscientiously
tried to find workable solutions to the problem presented by the conscription system. However, after noting the dissent and the various proposals
and counter-proposals, one is inevitably brought face to face with the
question, *Is* there a satisfactory alternative to the draft?

The answer seems to be no. There is no way by which a country
fighting a war can avoid ordering *some* of its men to crawl through
steaming jungles, wade through snake-infested, polluted rivers, and live
for weeks in mud-floored, sun-baked trenches. There is no way to avoid
exposing men to the tensions and dangers that break their nerves, their
spirits, and their bodies. There is no way to avoid the disease, the loss
of limbs, the blindness, the life-long crippling, and the death which

---

* Contributed by a veteran of World War II.

inevitably come to men who go to war. There is no way to eliminate the heartbreak of separation from loved ones, the disruption of life, the sacrifice of men's most vigorous and most treasured years. There is no way to avoid exposing some men to the dehumanizing experience of battle, where the law is the animal law of survival—kill or be killed. In short, war *is* a matter of "blood, sweat, and tears," and we cannot stop their flow by devising new methods of selecting men to go into battle.

What, then, is the answer? Quite clearly, the only solution that is truly satisfactory is to create a world in which a draft will no longer be necessary—because there will be no need for armies. Such a world will come into existence only when men have learned to love more and hate less, when iron and bamboo curtains have come down, when there is understanding, trust, and cooperation among nations. It will come only when countries are no longer known as the have's and the have-not's; when we root out the misery of poverty, illiteracy, and disease. It will come only when nations put the desire for peace and the well-being of human beings above the thirst for power, for wealth, or for the spreading of a political ideology. It will come only when men no longer are motivated by a narrow nationalism or super-patriotism, when men no longer think of themselves as American citizens, Russians citizens, or Chinese citizens, but as citizens of the world. In other words, our only hope is that at some time we will remember that national boundaries are artificial barriers separating men from one another, and that, whether men be black or white or yellow, Russian, American, or Chinese, they share a kinship as members of the human race. They have the same needs, desires, and emotions; they have the same human capacity for nobility or meanness. They are all brothers on this minute speck in the universe, and they must learn to act like brothers if they—and the planet itself—are to survive.

This is the only real "alternative" to the draft. It is clear that we are still a long way from realizing it, but there is hope. There is hope in the loud voices of dissent raised against war, in the work of the United Nations, in the efforts of educators and statesmen who are attempting to establish better communication and understanding among nations, and in the selfless devotion and charity of countless men and women who are concerned about their fellowmen in places ranging from the jungles of Africa to the mountains of Tibet. We can only pray that these first stirrings of activity will continue and grow until we achieve the ideal of "One World," when the lion shall indeed "lie down with the lamb" and the draft and all that it implies will be only a fact in history.

What Do You Think?

1. Can you think of additional evidence that we are making progress toward a time when we shall no longer have to be concerned about raising armies?

2. What do you think the average citizen can and should do to bring about conditions that will lead to universal peace?

ACTIVITIES FOR INVOLVEMENT

1. Take a poll of students in your school and their parents to determine what their opinions are concerning alternatives to the draft. The following form may be used:

	Yes	No	Status (Student or Parent)	Sex
Part I:				
1. Do you think that the draft should be continued in its present form?				
2. Do you think the draft should be continued but altered in some ways?				

Part II:

If you think the draft should be eliminated and some alternative substituted, indicate your choice by checking one of the following alternatives:

1. Universal Military Training ⎽⎽⎽⎽
2. National Service Corps ⎽⎽⎽⎽
3. All-Volunteer Army ⎽⎽⎽⎽
4. Random selection by lottery ⎽⎽⎽⎽

When all the results have been obtained, tabulate them in the following manner, keeping the responses of students and parents separate:

% All Students (or Parents)	% All Males	% All Females

When the survey has been completed, provide all students with the results as a basis for discussion.

2. Hold a round-table discussion in which persons favoring each of the positions designated in the poll form are represented. Participants should be given time to prepare their case; that is, they should have the opportunity to find thoughtful reasons and evidence for their position and arguments to refute the positions taken by others.

3. In several of the articles in this chapter, arguments were presented to show either that an all-voluntary army would be too costly or that it would not be too costly—that it would, indeed, be more economical. Perhaps

you can get some idea as to which of these views is correct by doing the following: Have every boy in your class give the teacher a slip of paper on which he has indicated the yearly salary he would have to be offered to induce him to volunteer for the armed forces. (It is not necessary that the students identify themselves.) Several members of the class can then determine the median salary indicated by the respondents.

After the results have been obtained and made known to the class, such questions as the following can be discussed:

a. Does the median salary arrived at in the class correspond to or differ radically from salaries suggested in the various articles?

b. How does the median salary compare with the salary now being paid to draftees?

c. If all men (approximately 523,000) now serving in Vietnam were paid the median salary arrived at in this class, what would the cost in salaries alone amount to? What proportion of the total cost of the war in Vietnam does this figure represent?

4. William James, in "The Moral Equivalent of War," offers an interesting commentary on man's aggressive nature and suggests outlets for this impulse other than war. More recently, John Fischer, in an article in *Harper's Magazine* for January 1966 entitled "Substitutes for Violence," has presented similar ideas, drawing examples from contemporary life. Assign each essay to two students and have them present their findings to the class.

5. Assuming that a system of national service were adopted, how would you answer the following questions:

a. What service—VISTA, Peace Corps, Job Corps, military service, etc.— would you select? Why?

b. Is it likely that the government can find useful, worthwhile assignments for the young people involved in national service?

c. Do you think such a system would be fair to all young men and (as Margaret Mead suggests) to young women, or would it result in inequities? Explain your answer.

d. Can you think of ways in which a system of national service could make valuable contributions to your community?

e. Do you think 18 or whenever a boy is graduated from high school is the best age at which to enlist young people into national service, or do you think some other age would be better? Explain. What do you think of allowing people to choose when they will serve at any time between 18 and 25?

Compare your responses to these questions with those of your classmates. What differences do you notice? Similarities? How would you explain these similarities and differences?

BIBLIOGRAPHY
For Further Study

Books

CARPER, JEAN · *Bitter Greetings: The Scandal of the Military Draft* · New York, N. Y.: Grossman Publishers, 1967.

CHAPMAN, BRUCE K. · *The Wrong Man in Uniform: Our Unfair and Obsolete Draft—and How We Can Replace It* · New York, N. Y.: Trident Press, 1967.

CURTI, MERLE · *The Roots of American Loyalty* · New York, N. Y.: Columbia Univ. Press, 1946.

DUGGAN, J. C. · *Legislative and Statutory Development of the Federal Concept of Conscription for Military Service* · Washington, D. C.: Catholic Univ. Press, 1946.

EBERLY, DONALD J., (ed.) · *A Profile of National Service* · 1966, Overseas Educational Service · Available from National Service Secretariat, 350 Lexington Avenue, New York.

EKIRCH, ARTHUR A. JR. · *The Civilian and the Military* · New York, N. Y.: Oxford Univ. Press, 1956.

EVERS, ALFRED · *Selective Service—A Guide to the Draft,* (rev. ed.) · Philadelphia, Pa.: J. B. Lippincott Co., 1963.

FELSEN, HENRY GREGOR · *To My Son in Uniform* · New York, N. Y.: Dodd, Mead & Co., 1966/1967.

FITZPATRICK, EDWARD A. · *Universal Military Training* · New York, N. Y.: McGraw-Hill Book Co., 1945.

LECKIE, ROBERT · *The Wars of America* · New York, N. Y.: Harper & Row, 1968.

MARMION, HARRY · *Selective Service in America: Conflict and Compromise* · New York, N. Y.: John Wiley & Sons, 1968.

MEYER, PETER · *The Pacifist Conscience* · New York, N. Y.: Holt, Rinehart & Winston, 1966.

SCHLISSEL, LILLIAN, (ed.) · *Conscience in America: A Documentary History of Conscientious Objection in America, 1757–1967* · New York, N. Y.: E. P. Dutton & Co., 1968.

STAFFORD, ROBERT T. *et al.* · *How To End the Draft: The Case for an All Volunteer Army* · Washington, D. C.: The National Press Inc., 1967.

SWOMLEY, JOHN M. · *The Military Establishment* · Boston, Mass.: Beacon Press, 1964.

TAX, SOL, (ed.) · *The Draft: A Handbook of Facts and Alternatives* · Chicago, Ill.: The Univ. of Chicago Press, 1967.

THOMAS, NORMAN · *Is Conscience a Crime?* · New York, N. Y.: Vanguard Press, 1927.

WILLENZ, JUNE A., (ed.) · *Dialogue on the Draft* · Washington, D. C.: American Veterans Committee, 1967.

Paperback Books and Pamphlets

BOULDING, KENNETH E. *et al.* · *The Draft* · New York, N. Y.: Hill and Wang Co., 1968. (A report prepared for the Peace Education Division of the American Friends Service Committee.)

FINN, JAMES, (ed.) · *A Conflict of Loyalties: The Case for Selective Conscientious Objection* · New York, N. Y.: Pegasus, 1968.

FULBRIGHT, J. WILLIAM · *The Arrogance of Power* · New York, N. Y.: Random House, 1966.

HARWOOD, MICHAEL, (ed.) · *The Student's Guide to Military Service* (Rev. ed.) · New York, N. Y.: Bantam Books, Inc., 1966.

"How Can the United States Best Maintain Manpower for an Effective Defense System?" · Compiled by the Legislative Reference Service, Library of Congress, 1968 Document No. 75, U. S. Government Printing Office, Washington, D. C.: 1968. (A collection of excerpts and a bibliography relating to the National High School Debate Topic 1968–69.)

In Place of War: An Inquiry into Nonviolent National Defense · Prepared by a working party of the American Friends Service Committee. New York, N. Y.: Grossman Publishers, 1967.

LEVY, A. · *The Draftee's Confidential Guide* · New York, N. Y.: The New American Library, 1967.

LYNN, CONRAD J. · *How to Stay Out of the Army: A Guide to Your Rights Under the Draft Law* · New York, N. Y.: Grove Press, 1967.

MILLER, JAMES C. III, (ed.) · *Why the Draft? The Case for a Volunteer Army* · Baltimore, Md.: Penguin Books, Inc., 1968.

MILLIS, WALTER · *Arms and Men: A Study in American Military History* · New York, N. Y.: The New American Library, 1956.

National Service Newsletter · Published monthly by the National Service Secretariat, 350 Lexington Avenue, New York, N. Y.

RAYMOND, JACK · *Your Military Obligations and Opportunity* (rev. ed.) · New York, N. Y.: The Macmillan Co., 1964.

Report of the Task Force on the Structure of the Selective Service System · Washington, D. C.: U. S. Government Printing Office, 1967.

STILLSON, ALBERT C. · *The Selective Service Act of 1967, A Survey of Proposals and Studies Concerning Its Revision and Replacement* · Washington, D. C.: The Library of Congress Legislative Reference Service, 1968.

The Selective Service System, Its Concept, History and Operation · The Office of Public Information, National Headquarters, Selective Service System, Washington, D. C., 1967.

WATERS, M. A. · *G I's and the Fight Against War* · New York, N. Y.: Merit Publishers, 1968.

Articles

CAMERON, GAIL · "Why 'Good' Sons Become Draft Dodgers," *Ladies Home Journal*, August 1967.

CLAUSEN, OLIVER · "Boys Without a Country," *The New York Times Magazine*, May 21, 1967.

DAVIDSON, BILL · "Hell, No, We Won't Go!" *The Saturday Evening Post*, January 27, 1968.

ESTY, JOHN C. JR. · "The Future of the Draft," *The Nation*, September 12, 1966.

GOODMAN, JEFFREY · "How to Be Patriotic and Live with Yourself," *Atlantic Monthly*, February 1966.

GOODMAN, WALTER · "They March to Different Drummers," *The New York Times Magazine*, June 26, 1966.

GRAUMAN, LAWRENCE JR. · "The Goals of Dissent," *The Nation*, December 11, 1967.

HATFIELD, MARK O. · "The Draft Should Be Abolished," *The Saturday Evening Post*, July 1, 1967.

JOHNSON, KEITH, R. · "Who Should Serve?" *Atlantic Monthly*, February 1966.

MARMION, HARRY A. · "Selective Service: Are There Any Alternatives?" *Educational Review*, Spring 1967.

NOLAN, MARTIN F · "Draft by Lottery," *New Republic*, July 30, 1966.

PHILLIPS, CABELL · "Your Best Deal in Military Service," *Harper's Magazine*, July 1957.

SANDERS, MARION K. · "The Case for National Service Corps," *The New York Times Magazine*, August 7, 1966.

STAR, JACK · "Our Draft Dodgers in Canada," *Look*, March 7, 1967.

"Students and the Draft: When Not All Serve," *Saturday Review*, April 15, 1967.

"The Case for a Volunteer Army" (Time Essay), *Time*, January 10, 1968.

"The Draft: Who, When, Why?" *Senior Scholastic*, September 28, 1967.

TYLER, GUS · "Dangers of a Professional Army," *New Leader*, April 24, 1967.

VELVEL, LAWRENCE R. · "Freedom of Speech and the Draft Card Burning Cases," *University of Kansas Law Review*, January 1968.

WILHELM, ROSS · "How to End the Draft," *The Nation,* November 15, 1965.

WOFFORD, HARRIS · "Toward a Draft Without Guns," *Saturday Review,* October 15, 1966.

WREN, CHRISTOPHER S. · "Vietnam: Pacifist on the Killing Ground," *Look,* December 26, 1967.

Films and Filmstrips

Action Vietnam (Big Picture Series) (TV 654; B/W; Department of the Army*) · Story of two American heroes in Vietnam.

Adjustment to Military Life (18 min; Department of the Army) · Shows the adjustments a trainee is required to make in his transition from civilian to military life, with emphasis on physical and moral standards.

America on the Move (Big Picture Series) (B/W; Department of the Army) · Documentary describing the spirit and the motivation of our country as it meets the challenge of today.

Boundary Lines (10 min; Princeton Film Center) · An animated short subject contending that people must learn to live in harmony if they are to survive; that separation of people for various reasons leads to fear, hatred, and finally war.

Brotherhood of Man (10 min; Princeton Film Center) · Animated color film on the subject of international tolerance and understanding.

Code of Conduct—Article I—Our Heritage (8 min; B/W; 1960) · Presents precepts of Article I which sets forth traditional spirit of the American soldier in the call of duty to defend his land. Department of the Army.

How Sleep the Brave (Big Picture Series) (TV 623; color; Department of the Army) · Poetic memorial to Americans who lived and struggled for American ideals and now rest in Arlington National Cemetery.

It's Your America (35 min; Princeton Film Center) · Tells the story of a young man who learned through the experience of war that the terms "freedom," "democracy," and "liberty" really mean.

Mary S. McDowell (From the Profiles in Courage series) (50 min; Saudek) · The story of a teacher in a New York high school who refused to sign a voluntary loyalty oath or engage in any activity which would aid the war effort.

Neighbors (9 min; National Film Board of Canada) · Parable of two men who, after living side by side peaceably, destroy each other over the possession of a flower that one day grows on their property line.

Now the Peace (20 min; Princeton Film Center) · A summary of the United Nations program for world security and the part which the individual can play in maintaining world peace.

---

* Department of the Army Films may be obtained by directing requests to Information Officer at the nearest Army Installation.

Physical Fitness (Big Picture Series) (TV 721; color; Department of the Army) · The future of America's fighting force is invested in the physically fit—the men and women with the strength and courage to protect her interests.

Preamble to Peace (Big Picture Series) (TV 373; B/W; Department of the Army) · Examination of the meaning of the United States Constitution and its Preamble.

Ready 'Round the World (Big Picture Series) (TV 717; color; Department of the Army) · In the cold reality of war both individual soldiers and nation are either ready or they are dead. Film speaks of men on guard around the world protecting the American way of life.

Something to Build On (Big Picture Series) (TV 688; color; Department of the Army) · What opportunities are available for the young man who makes a career of the United States Army.

The American Soldier in Combat (AIF No. 11; 29 min; B/W; 1960; Department of the Army) · An inspiring account of the combat history of the American soldier from the era of the American Revolution through the Korean War.

The History of Dissent (Filmstrip; The New York Times Book and Educational Division) · An examination of how dissent helped to shape American history, focusing on such figures and issues as Tom Paine, Thoreau, Joan Baez, anti-war protest, and draft riots in various wars.

The Pale Horsemen (20 min; Princeton Film Center) · A dramatic record of what happens to civilians caught in the fury of modern warfare and what nations can do to alleviate and prevent the suffering caused by war.

Time Out of War (22 min; Grove Press Film Library) · Winner of an Academy Award, this film comments on the insanity of war.

Time to Go (Selective Service; 28 min; Department of the Army) · Shows organization, purpose, and operation of Selective Service System; requirements, obligations, classification and deferment of the draftee, pre-induction processing, induction, and benefits of army training.

Your Stake in Tomorrow (RF No. 21–6; 20 min; B/W; 1965; Department of the Army) · Encourages high school graduates to enlist in the Army for career development; cites opportunities for specialist training.

Tapes

National Defense (HT 58; 15 min.; Pa. Dept. of Public Instruction *) · George Meany, president of the A. F. L.-C. I. O. describes the wish of the American labor group for peace but not the kind of a peace which would see a lessening of economic, political, or social stature for the United States.

---

* Pa. Dept. of Public Instruction tapes may be obtained through the audio-video Duplication Center, Bureau of Instructional Services, Department of Public Instruction, Room 321, Educational Building, Box 911, Harrisburg, Pa. 17126.

Our Inalienable Rights (HT 969; 15 min; Pa. Dept. of Public Instruction) · "Commerce; free thought; free press and free speech; personal freedom; trial by jury; conscience answerable only to God."

Anatomy of Peace (HT 820; 60 min; Pa. Dept. of Public Instruction) · Excerpts from speeches by Robert M. Hutchins, Hubert H. Humphrey, Adlai Stevenson, etc., on the possibilities for peace in the nuclear age.

The Most Important American (HT 690; 15 min; Pa. Dept. of Public Instruction) · "Freedom begins and ends in respect for the dignity and integrity of individual human beings. Therefore, every American is 'the most important American.'"

The Nature of Liberty—By Salvador DeMadariaga (20 min; McGraw-Hill Sound Seminars) · Describes the nature of a free man and of the society in which he lives.

The Warless World (HT 834; 60 min; Pa. Dept. of Public Instruction) · An interview discussing the implication of a warless world for a society that has never lived without the institution of war.

War and Peace (HT 949; 30 min; Pa. Dept. of Public Instruction) · Lecture by Dr. Hans Speier, Social Scientist and author, Chief of the Social Science Division of the Rand Corporation.